Gifts from
Grandpa's Workshop

THE
LILIAN S. BESORE
MEMORIAL LIBRARY
GREENCASTLE, PENNSYLVANIA
FOUNDED MARCH 20, 1963

Gifts from Grandpa's Workshop

Howard V. French

TAB BOOKS
Blue Ridge Summit, PA

FIRST EDITION
FIRST PRINTING

© 1991 by **TAB Books**.
TAB Books is a division of McGraw-Hill, Inc.

Library of Congress Cataloging-in-Publication Data

French, Howard V.
    Gifts from grandpa's workshop / by Howard V. French.
      p.   cm.
    Includes index.
    ISBN 0-8306-2139-3 (h)   ISBN 0-8306-2138-5 (p)

    1. Woodwork. I. Title.
  TT180.F74 1991
  684′.08—dc20   91-21715
                                             CIP

Acquisitions Editor: Stacy Varavvas-Pomeroy
Book Editor: April D. Nolan
Production: Katherine G. Brown
Book Design: Jaclyn J. Boone
Cover photo by Susan Riley, Harrisonburg, VA
Cover by Holberg Design, York, PA

Contents

Acknowledgments

I would like to thank my friend and mentor, David M. Camp, editor of *Popular Woodworking*, for his guidance, for his continuing support, and for encouraging me to compile the material for this book.

Introduction

Practically everyone enjoys exercising his or her abilities and skills in creating some worthwhile project, whether it is a gift, a toy, a decorative piece, or even some article of furniture. The sense of pride in accomplishment as your creations emerge from the chosen raw materials to become beautiful finished pieces is unbeatable.

This sense of satisfaction, this feeling of pride in such creations does not end here, of course. Handcrafted items are all the more prized as gifts because they *are* handcrafted. They also can be used or displayed with justifiable pride, and eventually handed down to others to be cherished and enjoyed.

In addition to being a most satisfying avocation—or vocation—good craftsmanship can become a source of added income. Another very real advantage comes into being when satisfied recipients and purchasers of your creations are motivated to send referral customers your way. Added remuneration thus generated can, and sometimes does, become quite substantial.

I am convinced that woodworking is an ideal craft medium through which to realize all these rewards, and by both men and women. This book was planned and has been compiled to help others, from the novice hobbyist to the skilled craftsman, realize even more from a most rewarding medium of expression—woodworking.

The beginning woodworker will be learning certain new and interesting procedures, along with an added vocabulary peculiar to this craft. (No, a *rabbet* is not a woodcraft creation with long ears.) I have attempted to start out with simpler, less involved projects in the earlier chapters of this book. I believe these projects will be both interesting and rewarding, nonetheless, while also leading you to more ably accomplish the projects of increasing complexity as you progress through this challenging series of designs.

Many of these exciting and enjoyable projects can be built with only minimal shop equipment and ordinary hand tools, and quite profitably. However, power tools can greatly reduce the time and effort needed to fabricate most project components. The precision inherent in the use of power tools can also assure the interchangeability of like parts, which is especially significant if you plan to make large quantities of the end items for commercial sale.

It usually takes more time to make a proper power tool setup (a special jig or fixture to facilitate cutting out a particular component) than it does to cut out that component. Therefore, you might find it logical to make several, or a *production run*, of a part before breaking down a particular setup. If you plan to do this, be sure to make a precise and durable pattern piece for that component rather than making a layout directly onto the material to be cut each time. Also, determine which pieces can be stacked, so that two or more thicknesses of material can be cut simultaneously.

Speaking of thicknesses, a word may be in order here regarding the currently available dimensioned lumber sizes. For instance, a stock 2-×-4 piece of lumber is not 2 inches thick and 4 inches wide, as the unitiated might very logically suppose. It came off the head rig at the sawmill in a two-inch thick slab, all right, but by the time it passed through the edger and the planer, it ended up being only $1^{1}/2$ inches thick and $3^{1}/2$ inches wide.

By the same token, a 1-×-12 piece of lumber ends up being, actually, $3/4$ inch thick × $11^{1}/4$ inches wide. We pay for the sawdust and the planer chips, too, but we have to make do with what is left. Standard lengths usually start at 8 feet, increasing in increments of 2 feet (within limits).

I have taken care in drafting all component parts of the projects contained in this book to utilize standard dimensioned lumber and plywood sizes which are to be found in almost any lumberyard or building supply store. Usually a fraction of an inch one way or another in a design won't make any appreciable difference in either looks or performance. However, it can make a considerable difference in waste materials created and, ultimately, in the cost of the finished item(s). Failure to take into account the width of the saw kerf alone can sometimes result in unnecessary scrap being left over from a project.

An illustrated glossary of certain terms peculiar to woodworking will be found at the end of this book. Another handy reference is the appendix, entitled "Shop Notes." In this section, several of the most popular lumber and materials sizes and styles are shown, along with their finished dimensions. I think this added information will be helpful, especially to those who are unfamiliar with buying and using materials for woodworking.

Once you have cut, shaped, or contoured a given component it should be sanded smoothly, and always with the grain. This should be done prior to final assembly and/or the application of whatever filler or sealer coat is in order. In fact, sanding (and in some instances shaping, sculpting, or engraving) of a project can make the difference between just a good completed item and a showpiece—a work of art.

You also must consider the strength of a finished project in relationship to the stresses that might be brought to bear upon it in normal use. This must be anticipated and provided for. The choice of woods, the direction of the grain(s), and the design features incorporated can make a difference. Attractive and/or unusual grain patterns can be revealed or enhanced during the final finishing process.

Purely decorative items, where strength and weight are not of significant importance and where the final finish is to be pigmented (paint, enamel, etc.), can often be made from the lightest and least expensive materials and still win a prize at the county fair or craft show.

Additional woodworking patterns are featured, along with illustrations and construction details, in many current craft and trade magazines. Some of the projects contained in this book have been featured in *Popular Woodworking* Magazine.

Several excellent books featuring a variety of interesting and worthwhile projects in woodworking and other crafts are available from TAB Books.

1
El Gato

El Gato (the cat) is easy to make and is certain to be a conversation piece wherever he is displayed. Just follow the detailed drawings, along with the pertinent shop notes, to create a project that is both attractive and useful. El Gato will tirelessly hold your necklaces, bracelets, pencils, napkins, or letters. He is also clean, quiet, and housebroken (FIG. 1-1).

INSTRUCTIONS

Start making this little fellow by laying out a pair of leg pieces (A), as shown in FIG. 1-2. Note that both front and back leg pieces are identical, so two of these are required per assembly. Lay out a 1/2-inch grid pattern on heavy paper or cardboard at least 4 inches wide by 9 inches long. Transfer the leg outlines onto your grid pattern and cut it out, following the heavier lines. Trace around these outlines onto your chosen material.

Follow the same procedure to lay out a head piece, as shown in FIG. 1-3. This can be done within a 4-inch-×-4-inch square. The tail component can be laid out from the dimensions given in FIG. 1-4, either onto pattern paper or directly onto the chosen wood. Blend the connecting radii smoothly while maintaining a uniform 3/4-inch width.

The body parts are easy to lay out with a compass because they are 3-inch diameter circles. Two to four of these are required per assembly, depending on the overall body length desired in the completed project.

All these components can be cut from 3/4-inch white pine lumber, or almost any other available 3/4-inch material. Most shops already have more than enough scrap lumber on hand to make one (or more) of these items. Stay just outside the pattern or layout lines when cutting out these parts so that they can be sanded to size later.

ASSEMBLY

Once you have cut out all the necessary components, stack the body parts (2 to 4 each), and check for their *concentricity*, which means sharing a common centerline, with their circumferences generally conformed. Sand their mating surfaces smooth. These parts can now be glued and *finish-nailed* (secured together

El Gato

Materials List

No. Req.	Part	Name	Thick	Wide	Long	Remarks
2	A	Legs	3/4"	31/2"	81/4"	White pine or (?)
2-4	B	Body	3/4"	3" dia.		
1	C	Head	3/4"	39/16"	31/2"	
1	D	Tail	3/4"	11/4"	6"	
1	E	Base (optional)	1/4"	41/2"	41/2"	Plywood or Masonite

Hardware & Supplies

	Felt, 1/16" × 41/2" × 41/2"	Optional
2	Eyes, approximately 3/8" diameter	
1	Nose, approximately 3/8" wide	
1	Bell, approximately 1/2"	
	Ribbon, 1 foot	

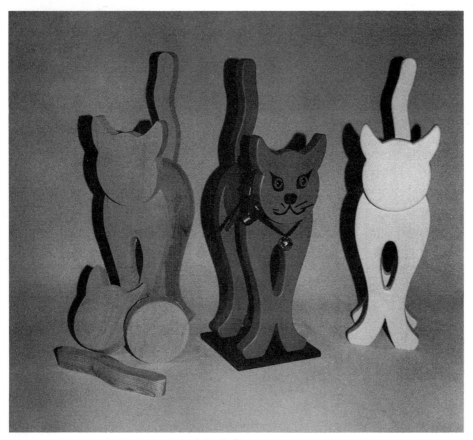

1-1 El Gato.

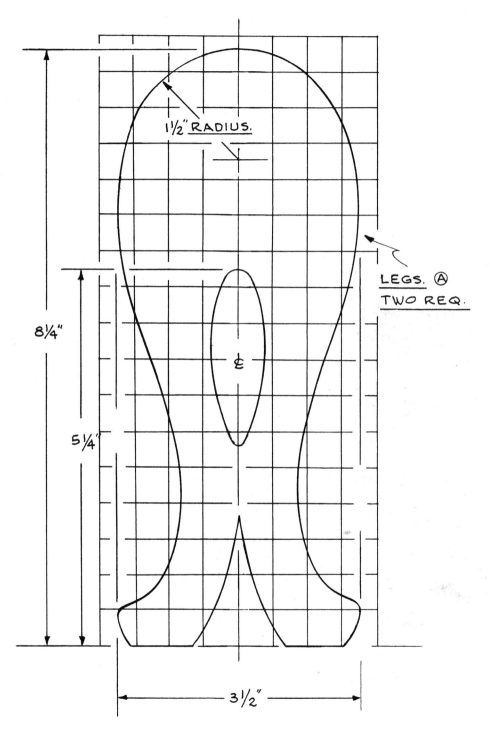

1½" RADIUS.

8¼"

5¼"

LEGS. Ⓐ
TWO REQ.

℄

3½"

1-2 Start making El Gato by laying out a pair of leg pieces.

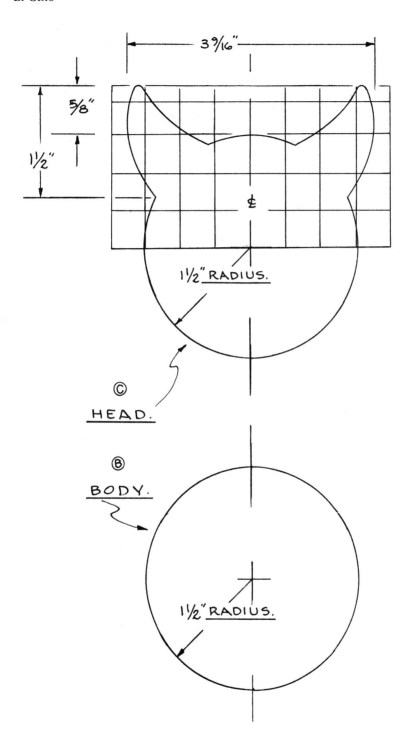

3 9/16"

5/8"

1 1/2"

₵

1 1/2" RADIUS.

©

HEAD.

®

BODY.

1 1/2" RADIUS.

1-3 Follow the same procedure to lay out a head piece.

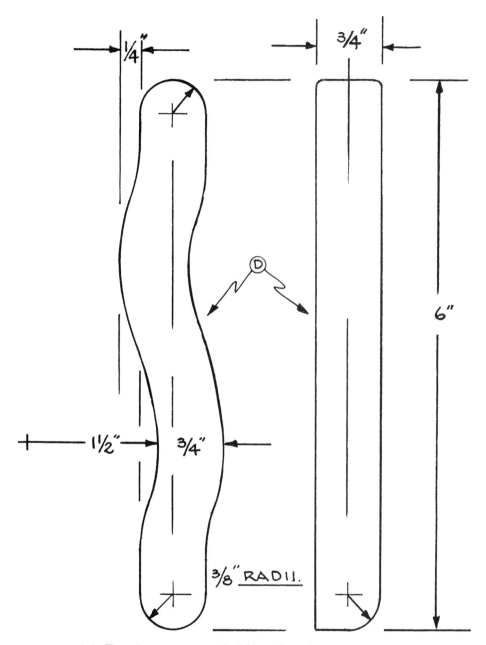

1-4 The tail component can be laid out from the dimensions given.

with small finishing nails). When this is done, sand their circumferences into smooth and cylindrical conformity.

Sand the mating surfaces of the two leg parts, and place the finished body subassembly between them, as shown in FIG. 1-5. Glue and finish-nail these components together, making certain that correct alignment is maintained.

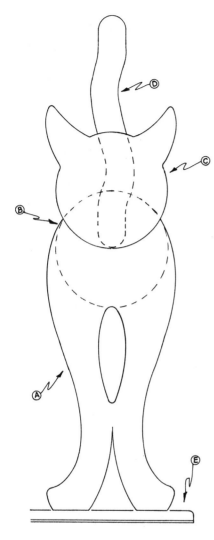

1-5 Sand the mating surfaces of the two leg parts and place the finished body subassembly between them. Locate the head and tail parts.

Locate the head and tail parts as shown in FIG. 1-5. Sand their surfaces appropriately and glue and finish-nail them into place to complete the total assembly. Fine-sand the entire project in preparation for whatever final finish coat is to be applied. Finely sand all the exposed sharp corners until they are smooth.

A mounting base piece is optional. Such a base will provide additional stability, depending upon the service expected of El Gato. The original project was mounted on a 1/4-inch×-41/2-inch-×-41/2-inch base since it contains three body parts. More, or fewer, body parts will alter the length of such a base by 3/4 inch per part.

FINISHING

The prototype project was finished in three successive coats of a flat, medium gray enamel, lightly sanded between coats. The base piece was sanded and finished in a green enamel, then glued and finish-nailed to each of the four feet. Finally, a piece of $^1/_{16}$-inch green felt was glued to the bottom and trimmed for a net fit.

The project could very well be declared complete at this point, unless you want further finishing details. You can buy cat eyes and nose pieces in various sizes from most hobby and craft supply stores. The prototype was fitted with these, along with a bright ribbon collar and a small bell. Small sprigs were driven in to simulate whiskers, bent appropriately, and painted flat black. Flat black "eye liner" was also applied. Such finishing details make for greater realism, but are certainly optional.

El Gato is now ready to assume his place in the household as a showpiece or as a welcome gift. In any event, he will be a faithful servant and a lovable pet.

2
Goose candy container

This graceful goose design candy container holds a generous supply of your favorite hard candies, M&M's, gum balls, or other goodies. The clear plastic wings make it easy to see at a glance what is in store. The colors of the contents or their wrappings can serve to carry whatever holiday motif.

This is a fun project which is easy to make. Almost any sound 2 × 12 lumber will suffice, especially if you plan to paint the completed unit. If the material you choose has an interesting grain pattern, give some thought to preserving and enhancing it with a clear finish. Either way, it will be an attractive showpiece.

INSTRUCTIONS

Please read completely through this section before starting any cutting operations.

Lay out a pattern piece for both the body and the wing components by referring to FIGS. 2-2 and 2-3. Transfer the body pattern onto the chosen wood to establish the body outline so that the grain generally follows the angle of the goose's neck. Note that the 1/2-inch squares which describe the body cavity are indicated by diagonal lines as well. Cut out this area later.

Locate the eye and pilot-drill through the material with a small diameter drill bit at this point. Follow the pilot hole from either side with a 1/4-inch "paddle blade" bit, but to no more than 1 inch in depth. Now turn the material over and drill through from the other side to intercept this hole. Following this procedure will leave a clean, splinter-free hole on both surfaces.

In like manner, locate and pilot-drill a small hole through the aft end of the body cavity, as indicated in FIG. 2-3. Follow this pilot hole with a 7/8-inch-diameter paddle blade bit or a Forstner bit. Note the third hole location indicated at the back of the goose's neck. Also make any short radius cuts in the same manner as outlined for the eye and the body cavity holes.

Cut out the body outline with a jigsaw or a narrow blade band saw. Notice that the fore and aft ends of the lid piece have been indicated by parallel lines at these locations (FIG. 2-3). Cut between the front pair of these lines to get into the body cavity, and cut it out. Now cut between the rear (hinge) pair of lines to free the lid component, using a very narrow saw blade. Too wide a kerf here will result

Goose Candy Container

Materials List

No. Req.	Part	Name	Thick	Wide	Long	Remarks
1	A	Body	$1^1/_2$"	$8^1/_2$"	$10^1/_2$"	Whitewood (SPF)
1	B	Lid	$1^1/_2$"	1"	$2^5/_8$"	
2	C	Wings	$^1/_8$"	$3^1/_8$"	$6^3/_4$"	Clear acrylic

Hardware & Supplies

1	Hinge, small brass
	Felt, $^1/_{16}$" × $1^1/_2$" × $2^3/_8$"
2	Beads, $^1/_4$" diameter, smooth dark Optional
	Ribbon

2-1 Goose candy container.

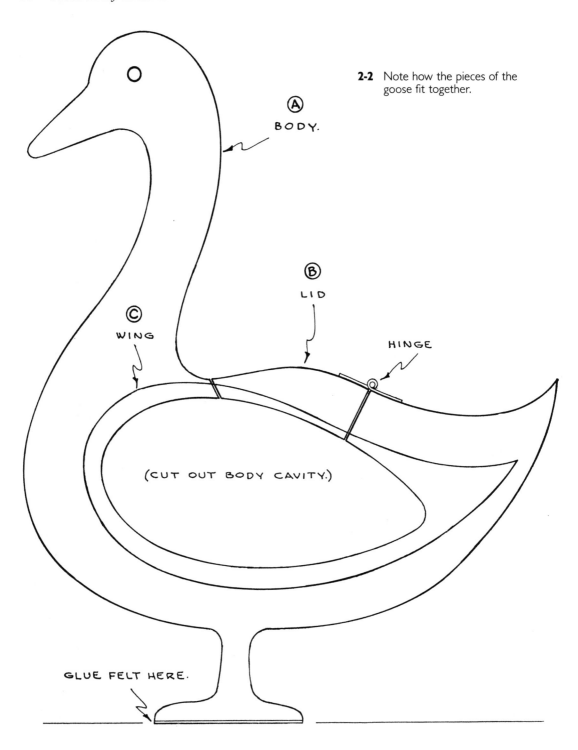

Ⓐ
BODY.

2-2 Note how the pieces of the goose fit together.

Ⓑ
LID

HINGE

Ⓒ
WING

(CUT OUT BODY CAVITY.)

GLUE FELT HERE.

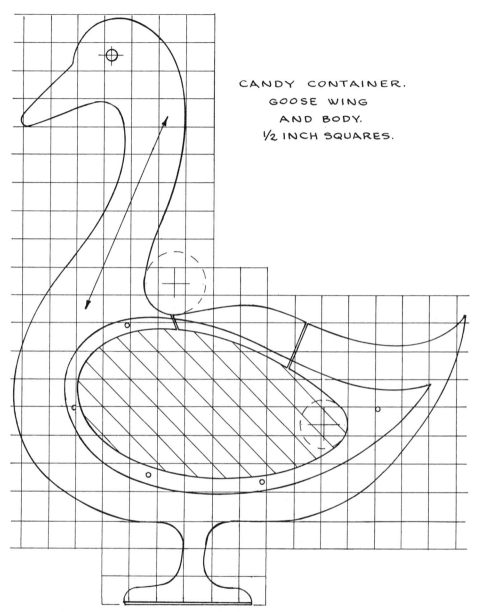

CANDY CONTAINER.
GOOSE WING
AND BODY.
½ INCH SQUARES.

2-3 Lay out a pattern piece for both the body and the wing components.

in a poor lid fit. You can remedy this condition, however, by gluing a small layer of felt to the aft surface of the lid opening and trimming it for a net fit.

SANDING

Small diameter drum-type sanders, chucked into a drill press, make it easier to sand the continuously curving outlines of the goose's body, inside and out. Use a coarse grit sandpaper to smooth out any obvious irregularities. Follow up with a fine grit to obtain a smooth surface all around. Sand the lid piece to leave it slightly thinner than the body (1¹/2-inches). Remember, the lid must be free to move between the two wings parts, to be installed later.

A smooth, ripple-free finish on the flat surfaces is especially desirable if the wood grain pattern is to be clear-gloss-finished. Secure a sheet of sandpaper to the saw table (or other smooth surface) by means of double-stick tape. Now press the surface of the workpiece against the grit, and use a back-and-forth sanding motion, always with the grain. Sand all corners until they are smooth and rounded.

WINGS

Clear acrylic material (Plexiglas, Lucite, etc.) should be cut with a fine-tooth blade and at slower cutting speeds to avoid generating too much heat. Also, use care when sanding the edges of the ¹/8-inch-thick wings for the same reason. Be careful to blow any emery or sanding dust from unprotected surfaces to avoid scratching: Do not attempt to wipe it off.

Lay the wing pieces over the body cavity, right and left. Equalize their overlapping margins, and mark the locations for the attaching holes (FIG. 2-3). Wire brads, 18 × ¹/2-inch, can be used to attach the wings, unless you want a more decorative head. Use an 18 × 1-inch wire brad as a drill bit, and drill through the wings at the marked hole locations and on into the wood, slightly.

Once this is done, make a very shallow countersink into these holes on the wings, on the outside surfaces only, to accommodate the heads of the brads. Mark the wings ''right'' and ''left'' and lay them aside for now.

FINISHING

If you want a *pigmented* (color) finish, you might need to apply a filler to the wood first, especially to any porous edges. Let the filler dry, and sand lightly between this and successive color coats until you achieve the desired finish. In the case of clear finish, the coating itself will become the ''filler.'' Again, fine-sand all surfaces lightly between successive coats. Finish the lid piece via the same process as for the body.

FINAL ASSEMBLY

Lay the finished body part on its side and on a clean, flat work surface. Align the appropriate wing part, and start the retaining brads into the pre-drilled holes. I've found that the drill press is an excellent ''brad set'' for this job. Just chuck a small common nail, head down, and use it as a set to press each brad flush. Do not overstress the plastic wing or breakage might result. Turn the body over and, with a clean shop towel under the newly installed wing, repeat this process with the remaining wing.

The lid piece can now be installed with a small hinge, to be located on its aft end as shown in FIG. 2-3. These usually come with sufficient small nails to install them. Again, the drill press will easily and steadily drive them into place securely.

Glue a small rectangle of felt onto the bottom of the foot. Two $1/4$-inch-diameter smooth glass beads pressed into the eye openings right and left will add a touch of realism.

About all that remains is to tie a colorful bow of ribbon around the goose's neck, and fill it up with your favorite sweet treats.

3
Chicken bookends

This comparatively simple design makes for an easy weekend project. Being both useful and attractive, it is guaranteed to please the young ones for whom it was originally created.

The bookends can be finished in a number of authentic chicken colorings to fit in with almost any decor (FIG. 3-1). If your chosen wood has an interesting grain pattern, you could finish it in clear. If a different color tone is important, you can stain the completed item first and then apply clear finish coatings.

INSTRUCTIONS

First, lay out a grid pattern of $1/2$ inch squares on a piece of heavy paper or cardboard, following the chicken outline shown in FIG. 3-2. Transfer this design onto your grid.

The broken lines shown in FIG. 3-2 are guides for optional detailing during final finishing. Two of these chicken body pieces are required per assembly. It might be possible to stack two thicknesses of the chosen material so you can band-saw or jigsaw them out simultaneously. In any event, cut just outside the pattern outline so that the pieces can be sanded to conformity later.

Locate the centers for the five $1/2$-inch-diameter holes with a sharp center punch. Whether or not the chicken bodies are stacked during the cutting operation, they must be stacked while line-drilling these holes through both pieces to ensure easy adjustment of the bookends.

Good shop practice when line-drilling two or more workpieces is to securely clamp them together with a flat piece of scrap material underneath. This will prevent the drill bit from splintering out the holes as it progresses through the desired parts and into the scrap piece. Drill through the hole centers first with a $1/8$-inch-diameter pilot drill. The pilot hole will then guide the $1/2$-inch bit, preventing any drift. Drill the $1/4$-inch-diameter eyeholes at this time, too.

Dowel rod stock is not always of a uniform diameter. It might even vary at different places along the same length of rod. A net fit is desired in only one of the body pieces. Make sure that a free slip-fit is maintained in the holes through the *mating* (movable) body piece, allowing for the thickness of later finish coatings to

Chicken Bookends

Materials List

No. Req.	Part	Name	Thick	Wide	Long	Remarks
2	A	Body	3/4 "	6¹/8 "	8¹/4 "	
5	B	Dowel rods	¹/2 " dia.		11 "	

Supplies

2	¹/16 " felt, ³/4 " × 3 "

be applied. This can be done by drilling through with a slightly larger diameter bit, or by hand-sanding the dowel rod pieces as necessary.

SANDING

Sand all outside surfaces of the two body pieces smoothly. Relieve all sharp edges by fine-sanding. In the same manner, relieve the sharp circumferences of the ¹/2-inch holes in the movable body piece and on both surfaces. Dress up the ¹/4-inch eyeholes by lightly touching them with a countersink bit.

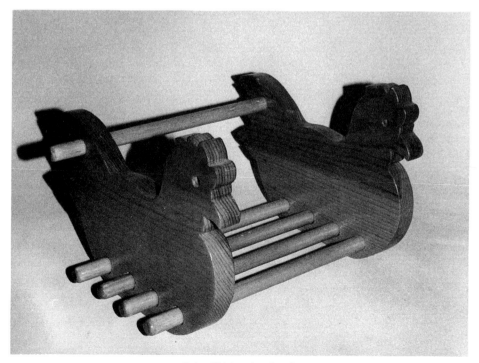

3-1 Chicken bookends.

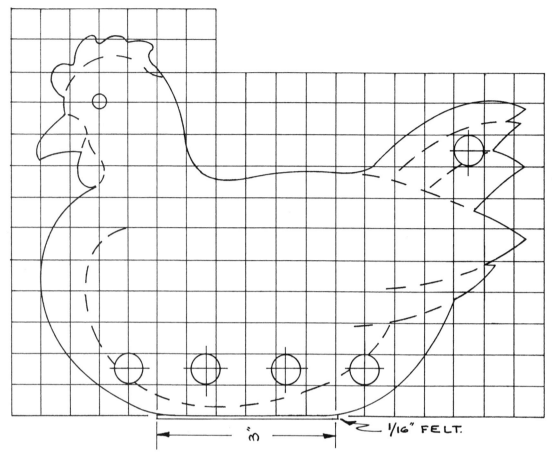

3-2 Lay out a grid pattern of 1/2 inch squares on a piece of heavy paper or cardboard, following the chicken outline.

DOWEL RODS

Cut the five pieces of 1/2-inch-diameter dowel rod to 11 inches in length. If you want a longer base (for larger books) this length can be increased, as the combined strength of the rods will support a substantial weight. Once five pieces of equal length will have been cut, turn or sand a spherical radius on both ends of each piece.

FINAL ASSEMBLY

Choose which surfaces of the chicken body pieces are to be exposed (outside). Now push all five of the dowel rods into their respective holes in the piece that is to remain fixed, and so that one end of each piece protrudes 1/4 inch through the outside surface, as shown in FIG. 3-3.

Before securing the rods in place, fit the slideable piece onto the free ends of

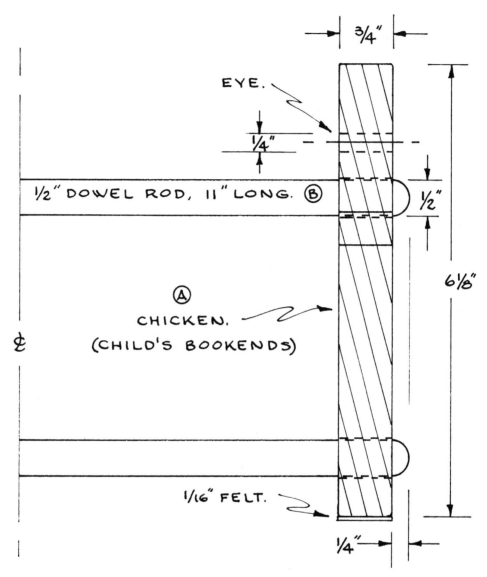

3-3 Push all five of the dowel rods into their respective holes so that one end of each piece protrudes 1/4 inch through the outside surfaces.

the rods to check for proper fit and movement. On the prototype projects, 18 ×-1-inch wire brads were used to secure the fixed ends in place. One such brad was used as a drill bit to pilot-drill through from the bottom and into the four lower rod ends. The top rod end was reached through the "tail feathers" (FIG. 3-2). This makes nailing and setting the brads in place much easier, especially when working with hardwoods.

FINISHING

In one prototype project, I left the natural wood grain exposed via a clear finish, without staining. This is an easy option if you want to achieve a Country or Early American look. The design indicated by the broken lines on FIG. 3-2 can be transferred onto the body pieces with fine black lines for a bit more detail.

I finished another prototype in gloss white enamel completely. Once this was dry, I transferred the detail markings onto the white outside surfaces in black enamel, then filled in the beaks with yellow and the combs and wattles with red. Be careful to maintain neat color separations if you use this final finishing touch.

All that remains is to glue the two strips of felt onto the bottom surfaces of the chicken bodies as shown in both FIGS. 3-2 and 3-3. Place the books on the four lower rods, next to the stationary chicken, and against the upper (rear) rod. Slide the moveable chicken figure up into position against the books. It will remain securely, until purposely moved to a new position.

4

3-D potted tulip

These colorful and decorative potted tulips are highly prized as gifts and will brighten up any area in which they are displayed. An alternative configuration of the tulips allows them to be "planted" among existing floral displays, indoors or outdoors.

Because the grain of the wood components does not show in the finished items, almost any inexpensive and readily available wood will suffice for their construction—just so that it will turn easily and sand smoothly (FIG. 4-1).

TURNING THE POTS

Start this project by turning the pots, (FIG. 4-2A), on your lathe. Several pots can be turned from a length of standard 4-×-4 ($3^1/2$ inches × $3^1/2$ inches) stock; however, it's about as fast and easy just to turn one pot at a time.

First, set up your bench saw to its maximum depth of cut, assuming you have a conventional ten-inch, tilt-arbor saw. You will probably have to make a second pass through the blade in order to sever the $3^1/2$-inch lengths off your material. Cut several such cubes while you are at it, then tilt the blade for a 45-degree-miter cut for the next operation.

Locate the centers on both ends of each piece as shown in FIG. 4-3 and center-punch them. Set the rip fence at $2^1/2$ inches from the saw blade, and remove all four corners of each piece as shown. This greatly minimizes the turning work necessary to convert these blank sections into pots, following FIG. 4-4. It is not necessary to leave a smooth surface on the bottoms of the pots or on their tops, other than the rim portions which will be exposed.

Sand the exposed surfaces of the pots smooth while they are still in the lathe. Drill a $1/4$-inch diameter hole in the top center of each pot, $5/8$-inch in depth. The pots are now ready for painting.

TURNING THE TULIPS

Material for the tulip pieces (FIG. 4-2B) can be ripped from scrap stock, $1^1/2$ inches × $1^1/2$ inches. Locate the centers on the ends of these pieces and turn them to

3-D Potted Tulip

Materials List

No. Req.	Part	Name	Thick	Wide	Long	Remarks
1	A	Pot	3¹/2″ dia.		3¹/2″	Turn from 4 × 4
1	B	Tulip	1¹/2″ dia.		1³/4″	
3	C	Foliage	5/8″	1¹³/16″	8″	
1	D	Stem	1/4″ dia.		9″	Dowel rod

Supplies

1	1/16″ Felt, 2¹/2″ diameter (pot bottoms)
3	Straight pins or wire brads (stamens)

Alternate Configuration

1	B	Tulip
3	C	Foliage
1	D	Stem (12″ long)

Supplies

3	Straight pins or wire brads (stamens)

4-1 3-D potted tulip.

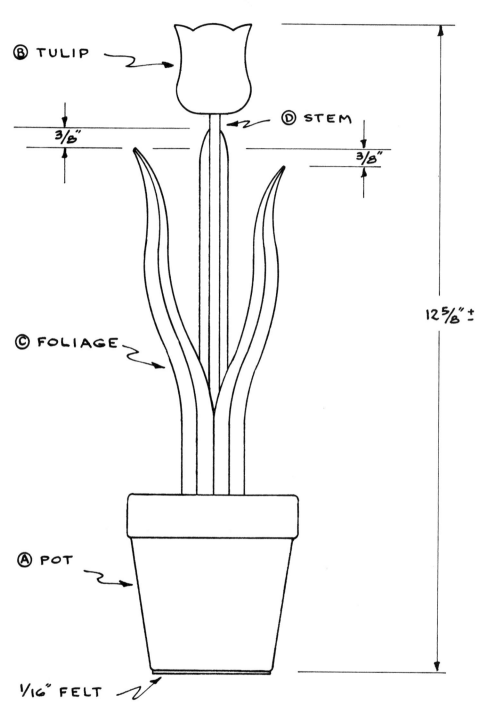

Ⓑ TULIP

Ⓓ STEM

3/8"

3/8"

Ⓒ FOLIAGE

12⅝" ±

Ⓐ POT

1/16" FELT

4-2 Material for tulip pieces can be cut from scrap.

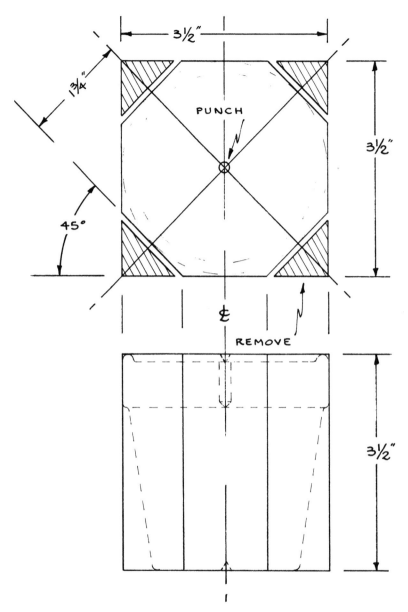

4-3 Locate and center-punch both ends of each piece.

$1^1/2$-inch-diameter rods. Mark off increments of $1^3/4$ inches for each tulip, leaving sufficient space between them to round off their bottom ends and to turn the concave top ends. Sand them while in the lathe, then remove and part them with your bench saw—very carefully (FIG. 4-5).

To make a jig for completing the tulip pieces, drill a $1^1/2$-inch-diameter hole into a block of scrap stock to a depth of $1^3/4$ inches. Because hole saws are not usually this deep, a paddle blade bit will do very nicely. Drill a $1/4$-inch hole

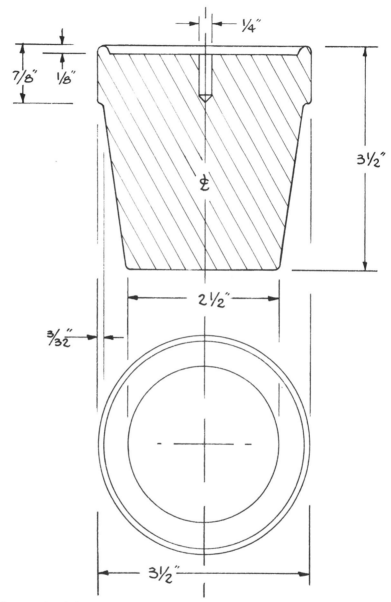

4-4 When turning, it is not necessary to leave a smooth surface on the bottoms or tops of the pots.

through the centerline of the jig piece, following the hole left by the pilot point of the paddle blade bit. This jig will make it easy to locate and drill the 1/4-inch × 3/8-inch hole in the bottom of each tulip. The same jig will hold the tulip while countersinking the top center of each, under your drill press.

Simulate petal divisions by making smooth V cuts at 90-degree intervals around the top using a sharp knife. Sand these cuts smooth with an emery board.

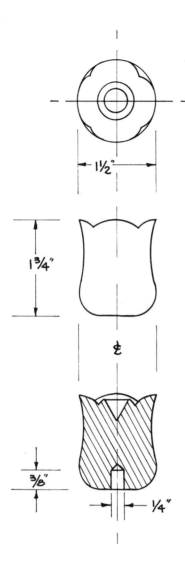

4-5 Mark off increments of 1³/4 inches for each tulip, leaving sufficient space between them to radius their bottom ends.

Press three ordinary pins or small wire brads into the center of each blossom to simulate stamens; then spread them slightly apart. The tulips are now ready for painting.

THE FOLIAGE

Lay out a pattern piece for the foliage components shown in FIG. 4-6C. Cut the pieces from ⁵/8-inch thick stock as shown, using a band saw or scroll saw. Make a set-up to either miter cut, or disc sand, the 30-degree flats on the lower ends of pieces (FIG. 4-6C) and to shape their top ends. Sand the finished foliage pieces smooth.

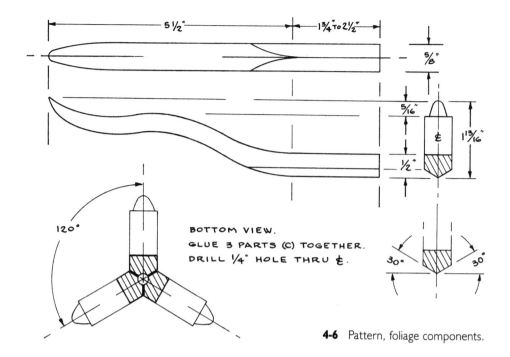

4-6 Pattern, foliage components.

SUBASSEMBLY

Apply glue to the 30-degree flats and press the foliage pieces together in threes, staggering their tops a bit for greater realism. Rubber bands will hold them securely while the glue sets up.

Next, square the bottom ends of these subassemblies and drill a $^1/_4$-inch hole through along their common centerline. Insert a 9-inch length of $^1/_4$-inch-diameter dowel rod through this hole so that $^5/_8$ inch of it extends past the bottom. Glue it into position. Mask off this $^5/_8$-inch portion of the rod (FIG. 4-6D), and also the top $^3/_8$-inch of the stem. These components are now ready for painting.

PAINTING

Paint the completed foliage/stem components in a suitable shade of green. If you choose bright yellow for the tulips, choose a contrasting color (brown, red, etc. for its pot); obviously, the same goes for red tulips, etc. Using a cotton swab as a brush, touch the tops of the simulated stamens with a contrasting color. It is not necessary to paint the bottoms of the pots or the tops—except for their rims.

FINAL ASSEMBLY

Final assembly is easy, once the several components are finished, painted, and dry. Remove the masking tape from the top and bottom of each stem. Apply a small amount of glue to the lower $^5/_8$-inch portion of the stem and to the bottom of the foliage pieces. Press the stem into the $^1/_4$-inch hole in the top of the pot. Put a droplet of glue into the hole in the bottom of the tulip and press it onto the top of the stem.

Using a small glue brush, "paint" the top of the pot with wood glue—from the base of the foliage to the rim. Sprinkle clean sawdust onto the wet glue to simulate potting soil. Finally, glue a 2¹/₂-inch circle of ¹/₁₆-inch felt to the bottom surface of each pot, as shown in FIG. 4-1.

ALTERNATIVE CONFIGURATION

You might want to leave off the pots on some creations, and extend the length of the stem pieces (FIG. 4-6D) to about three inches below the base of the foliage pieces (FIG. 4-6C). Such flowers may then be stuck into the soil of whatever greenery to further brighten any bed, planter, arrangement, or pot—indoors or outdoors.

5

Large pot trellis

This practical and very attractive design is intended for use in larger pots or in planters. It will support larger standing specimens and/or climbing varieties while showing them off to their best advantage. This artistic trellis will enhance the value of any plant—whether it is being offered for sale, being displayed in a decorative capacity, or presented as an exceptional gift item.

Almost any straight-grained, sound woods are adequate for making the component parts. Scrap pieces as short as 4 inches in length can be used (see the Materials List for this project). A total of about 21 feet of $5/8$-inch × $5/16$-inch material will be required per unit, along with a little over two feet of $5/8$-inch × $5/8$-inch material. The optional heart design pieces are cut from $1/8$-inch Masonite and add considerably to the attractiveness of the finished trellis assembly (FIGS. 5-1 and 5-2).

INSTRUCTIONS

Set the rip fence on your bench saw for a $5/8$-inch width of cut. A sharp planer blade will leave sufficiently smooth surfaces so that minimal sanding will be required later. Rip up enough stock to provide for whatever total number of units you plan to construct. About 21 linear feet of $5/16$-inch × $5/8$-inch stock are required per unit. While the fence is still set at $5/8$-inch, cut two pieces $12^3/4$ inches long for the vertical support pieces. I used oak for these pieces in the prototype for greater strength and longer life when in contact with the soil. Make 15-degree bevel cuts on one end of each of these two pieces. This "sharpening" procedure will facilitate soil penetration later.

Beginning at $2^1/4$ inches from the opposite ends, cut a radius as shown in FIG. 5-2. This is best done against a disk or belt sander. These radii will minimize localization of stress when you bend the $5/16$-inch × $5/8$-inch × 18-inch pieces to their desired shape.

Next, set the rip fence for $5/16$-inch width of cut and rip the $5/16$-inch × $5/8$-inch stock as required. Cut this material into the lengths indicated in the Materials List. Sand all these components smooth.

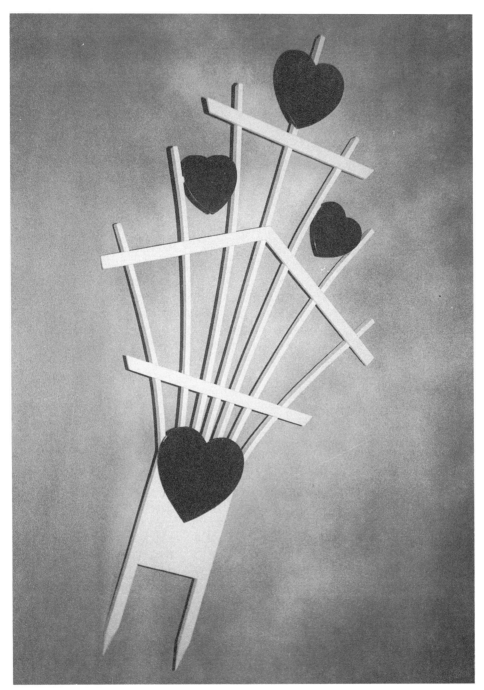

5-1 Large pot trellis.

Pot Trellis

Materials List

Part Name	No. Req. Per Unit	Thick	Wide	Long	Remarks
Vertical center	1	5/16"	5/8"	30"	20 1/2 feet of 5/16" × 5/8" mat'l. required.
Vertical curved	2	5/16"	5/8"	26"	
	2	5/16"	5/8"	22"	
	2	5/16"	5/8"	18"	
Vertical spacer	6	5/16"	5/8"	4"	
Cross pieces	2	5/16"	5/8"	3 1/8"	
	2	5/16"	5/8"	9 3/4"	
	1	5/16"	5/8"	10 1/2"	
	1	5/16"	5/8"	11 3/8"	
Vertical support pieces	2	5/8"	5/8"	12 3/4"	
Hearts	1	1/8"	5 1/4"	5 1/4"	Masonite
	1	1/8"	4"	4"	
	2	1/8"	3"	3"	

ASSEMBLY

Lay out a set of the vertical components in their correct order as shown in FIG. 5-2, starting with the 30-inch-long center piece. Apply glue to the mating surfaces (5/8 inch × 4 inches); the vertical pieces are joined together at their lower ends. Secure the successive laminations in place with #18 wire brads. Clamp the 11 middle pieces together, in parallel and in the same plane, between two pieces of scrap stock. Do not bring the clamps directly in contact with the outermost 4-inch spacer pieces. Lay this subassembly aside until the glue has set properly.

Depending upon the wood you chose, it might be necessary to immerse the two 18-inch pieces in water for a time in order to safely and easily spread them apart. Clamp the subassembly securely to a 30-inch length of 2 × 4 so that the center (30-inch) piece lies along its centerline. Put a piece of flat scrap stock between the clamp and the work, and apply glue to the mating surfaces of the remaining 18-inch pieces, the outermost spacer pieces, and the two vertical support pieces (FIG. 5-2). Finish-nail them in place right and left and secure all 15 components with clamps before spreading them into their final configuration.

Spread the tops of the two 18-inch pieces so that each is 8 1/2 inches from the centerline. Temporarily clamp the ends to a spreader piece of scrap stock. Install the lower horizontal piece (11 3/8 inches) by centering it on the 30-inch piece at a point 15 3/8 inches above the pointed tips of the support pieces. Secure it in place with #18 × 3/4-inch wire brads, and to the two 18-inch pieces only.

Notice that the two center spreader pieces (9 3/4 inch) are mitered at 30 degrees where they meet at the centerline. Locate and install these next—first to

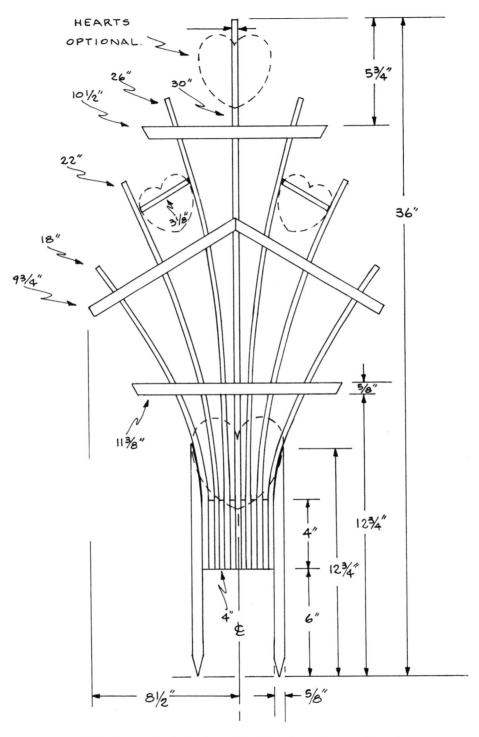

HEARTS
OPTIONAL.

26"
10½"
30"

22"
3/8"

18"

9¾"

5¾"

36"

5/8"

11⅜"

12¾"

4"

12¾"

4"
℄

6"

8½"

5/8"

5-2 Cut a radius beginning at 2¹/4 inches from the opposite ends.

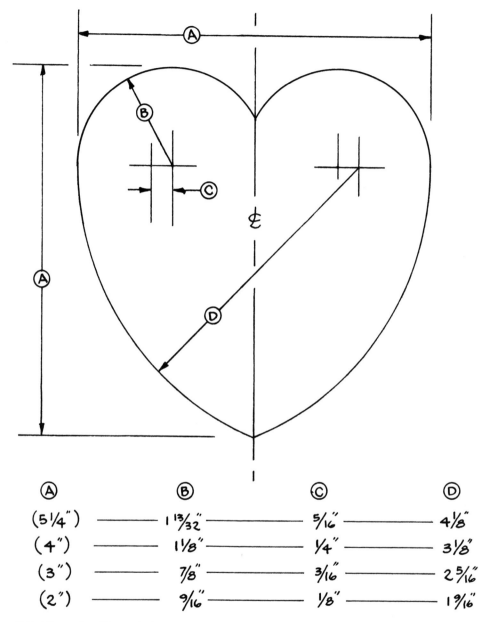

Ⓐ	Ⓑ	Ⓒ	Ⓓ
(5¼")	1 ¹³⁄₃₂"	⁵⁄₁₆"	4⅛"
(4")	1⅛"	¼"	3⅛"
(3")	⅞"	³⁄₁₆"	2⁵⁄₁₆"
(2")	⁹⁄₁₆"	⅛"	1⁹⁄₁₆"

5-3 The optional heart design pieces are cut from ¹⁄₈-inch Masonite and add considerably to the attractiveness of the finished trellis assembly.

the center piece, then to the 18-inch outside pieces. Temporarily insert the two 3¹⁄₈-inch pieces in place, right and left. At a point 5³⁄₄ inches down from the top, center the upper horizontal piece (10¹⁄₂ inches), and wire-brad it in place. Arrange the remaining intersections symmetrically right and left, maintaining graceful curvatures, and wire-brad all pieces securely. If necessary, apply a bit of glue to the ends of the two $3^1/_8$-inch spreader pieces before pressing their retaining brads into place. Leave the assembly thus clamped until the glue has set properly.

THE HEARTS

The optional decorative hearts are cut from $1/_8$-inch Masonite, as shown in FIGS. 5-1 and 5-3. Sand their edges smooth and lightly hand-sand their sharp corners. A $5^1/_4$-inch heart was made for the bottom of the prototype project, a 4-inch heart for the top, and two 3-inch hearts for the $3^1/_8$-inch spreader pieces right and left.

Spray the hearts with bright red gloss enamel in three successive coats, lightly sanding between coats. Spray the rest of the assembly with flat white enamel. Secure the finished hearts in place with #18 × $3/_4$-inch wire brads.

6

Flower pot hanger

This unique flower pot suspension project is fairly easy to make from readily available materials. It will accommodate a single pot, or it can be extended to display two pots—one below the other. In the latter instance, both the upper and lower rings are identical. Their distance apart is determined by the length of jack chain between them, and an easy and secure adjustment means is provided in the design (FIG. 6-1).

Standard materials are used, and the hardware is available at almost any hardware or building supply dealer. A jigsaw and a band saw can be put to good use in making this project.

INSTRUCTIONS

The main structural member in this design is the ring, which is cut from 3/4-inch exterior-grade plywood, as shown in FIG. 6-2. Unless you plan to make a number of these units at the same time, you don't really need a pattern piece.

Set your compass or dividers for a radius of 6^{1}/4-inches, and scribe a complete circle on the plywood material. Using the same center, scribe a concentric circle (having a radius of 4^{1}/4 inches) within the first circle. When you have cut out this ring or "doughnut" properly, you will have a 2-inch wide piece—8^{1}/2 inches inside diameter and 12^{1}/2 inches outside diameter.

At intervals of 120 degrees and 3/4 inch from the outer circumference, locate the centers for the three 1/2-inch-diameter holes. When drilling these holes through the plywood, be sure to place a flat piece of scrap stock under the hole locations so that the bit will leave a clean hole as it exits the ring.

Three of the support pieces are required per assembly. See FIGS. 6-3 and 6-4. Rip a piece of 2-x-4 stock (or any 1^{1}/2-inch material) 2^{1}/8 inches wide by about 6 inches in length. Lay out the support pieces as shown, leaving sufficient space between these layouts for the saw kerf. Jigsaw or band saw the 3/4-inch radii on one support piece at a time. Locate and drill the horizontal 1/2-inch hole on the centerline, at 1^{1}/8 inches from the end, and to a depth of 1^{1}/2 inches.

Set the bench saw blade for 1^{7}/8-inch depth of cut and make this cut at 1^{1}/2 inches from the end (bottom) of the support piece, and with the 1^{1}/2-inch (out-

Flower Pot Hanger

Materials List

Part Name	No. Req. Per Unit	Thick	Wide	Long	Remarks
Ring	1	3/4″	12 1/2″ dia.		Exterior-grade plywood
Pot support	3	1 3/4″	1 1/2″	2 1/8″	
Dowel rod	3	1/2″ diameter × 2 1/2-3″			1/2″ dowel rod stock
"S" hook	1	See article			
Jack chain		See article			

6-1 Hanging pot support.

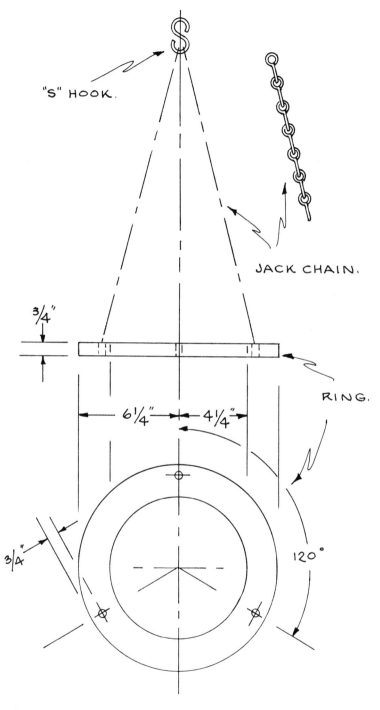

"S" HOOK.

JACK CHAIN.

3/4"

6 1/4" — 4 1/4"

RING.

3/4"

120°

6-2 The main structural member in this design is the ring, which is cut from 3/4-inch exterior grade plywood.

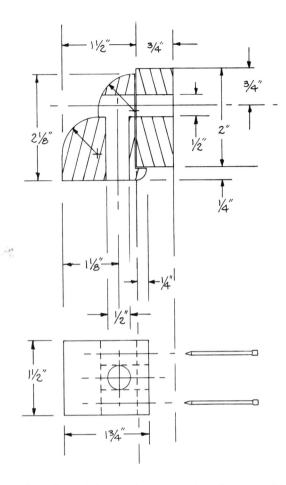

6-3 Three of the support pieces are required per assembly.

side) surface of the workpiece against the saw table (down). Next, rotate the work-piece 90 degrees on the table so that the $2^1/8$-inch surface is against the saw table (down), and cut the support piece free at its $1^3/4$-inch dimension. Break away the surplus material—with the grain—so that you leave a $1/4$-x-$1/4$-x-$1^1/2$-inch projection. Disregard the vertical $1/2$-inch-diameter holes for now.

Cut three pieces of $1/2$-inch-diameter dowel rod, $1^3/4$ to 2 inches in length. Check them for a slip fit within the horizontal holes in the support pieces. Drive a finish nail into the centerline in one end of each dowel piece so that the nail head extends $1/2$-inch, as shown in FIG. 6-5.

SANDING

Hand-sand the support pieces to general conformity with the curvature of the ring (FIG. 6-4). Sand all exposed surfaces smooth. Break the sharp corners by sanding a slight radius, except for the support pieces where they are to contact the ring's lower surface.

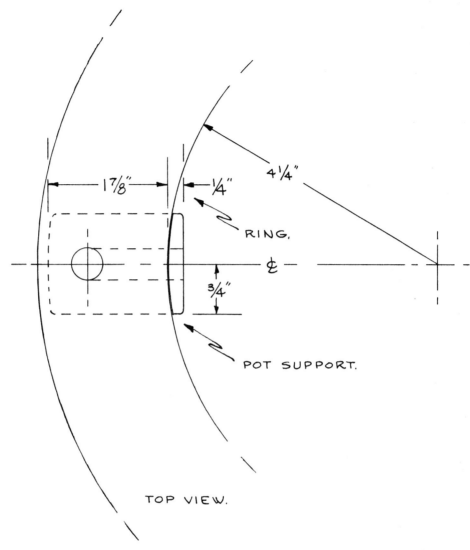

6-4 Hand-sand the support pieces to general conformity with the curvature of the ring.

SUBASSEMBLY

Locate the support pieces on the ring so that the centerlines of their horizontal holes will intersect the centerlines of the vertical $1/2$-inch diameter holes previously drilled through the ring. Chuck a finish nail into the hand drill as a bit, and pre-drill holes to a depth of no more than $3/4$ of the nail's length.

Apply glue to the mating surfaces and secure the support pieces in place with the finish nails. Once the glue has set properly, drill the three vertical holes

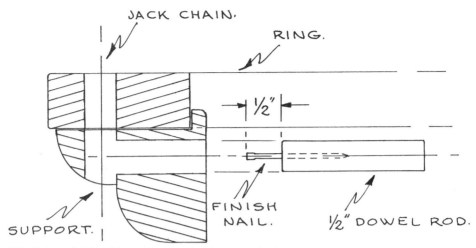

6-5   Drive a finish nail into the centerline in one end of each dowel piece so that the nail head extends 1/2 inch.

through the support pieces, using the holes previously drilled through the ring as guides. This assures the proper alignment and interception with the horizontal holes.

PAINTING

The prototype subassemblies were finished in gloss white enamel, but you might want to choose a shade of green to match the foliage of the plants you use. Apply successive coats of enamel, sanding lightly between coats.

The jack chain comes in gold or silver finishes, but you can enamel it, too, if desired.

FINAL ASSEMBLY

Choose an appropriate S hook, depending upon the weight it is to support. Determine the distance you need from the hook to the upper pot ring, and from the bottom of this pot to the top of the lower one (if two are to hang in series). In any event, leave about 6 inches of extra chain to hang below the lower ring to provide for future adjustment. Multiply this distance by three to determine the length of jack chain you need.

Secure one end of each chain length to the chosen S hook and close the bottom loop of the hook to prevent any inadvertent disconnection. Pass the three chains through the three vertical holes in the ring subassemblies. Count the links to be sure that all three chains are equal and that the ring will hang at the desired position. Insert the dowel pieces into the horizontal holes, nail-head first, so that the nails will pass through the desired links. A short piece of masking tape will adequately mark the chosen links.

Depending on the diameter of the pots to be supported, you might want to modify the lengths of the dowel rods so that they engage the circumference of the pot while remaining fully inserted into their horizontal holes. Once the pot is properly in place within a given ring, this becomes a "lock" against any inadvertent dislocation. Where a pot is merely tapered, with no pronounced lip or prominent rim to index the dowels beneath, you might want to slip 1/2-inch "crutch tips" over the inboard ends of the dowel pieces.

Obviously, the chain lengths can be adjusted fairly easily whenever you want to change plant or pot sizes and/or heights.

7
Bird feeder

This unique bird feeder is sure to become a popular meeting place for your feathered friends, once the word gets around. The feeder is a matching companion piece to the birdhouse in chapter 8, which features a fireplace and a woodpile on its porch.

The entire roof section of the feeder lifts up to allow easy access for filling. Parallel perches are provided, one on each side. A suspension hook, made from $3/16$-inch-diameter rod stock, makes it easy to hang the feeder and to take it down for refilling when necessary (FIG. 7-1).

INSTRUCTIONS

Study the two views of the feeder as shown in FIGS. 7-2 and 7-3. Identify all the components from the Materials List. I recommend that you read this chapter through before beginning construction, so you become familiar with the component parts as well as their relationship to each other. Note that in all the illustrations that follow, each piece is identified by the same letter. It is important for this project that you follow these letters (indicated in the Materials List); you might even want to mark the pieces with the appropriate letters for your reference.

Cut out the two identical end pieces from $3/4$-inch material as shown in FIG. 7-4. Lay out the locations (2) for the $1/2$-inch diameter holes and drill them to a depth of $1/2$-inch only. Make the $3/8$-inch × 1-inch rabbet cut along the bottom of each piece. These cuts will accommodate the perch support pieces later.

Set the rip fence on your bench saw at $3/16$ inch from the blade, and set the blade for $3/16$-inch depth of cut. Make the kerfs right and left on both pieces as shown. These are to accommodate the single-strength glass inserts, to be installed last. Following FIG. 7-5, note that the two $1/2$-inch holes, the $3/8$-inch × 1-inch rabbet cut, and the kerfs are all made on the same (inside) surfaces of the end pieces (A).

Using FIG. 7-6, note that the trough edge pieces (C), the feeder bottom (D), the roof section joiner (E) and the roof sections (F) all require making a 15-degree cut. Rather than changing the angle of cut several times, cut all these components first—excepting their 15-degree cuts. Start with the roof sections (F). Cut two pieces for each feeder, $5 1/4$ inches × 12 inches from $1/4$-inch tempered Masonite.

Cut the feeder bottom (D) from $1 1/2$-inch material, $5 5/8$ inches wide × $8 1/2$ inches long. Cut the roof joiner piece (E) from $3/4$-inch material, $3 3/4$ inches wide

Bird Feeder

Materials List

No. Req.	Part	Name	Thick	Wide	Long	Remarks
2	A	End pieces	$3/4$″	$7^3/16$″	$8^3/4$″	
2	B	Perch supports	$3/8$″	1″	10″	Hardwood
2	C	Trough edges	$3/8$″	1″	$8^1/2$″	Hardwood
1	D	Feeder bottom	$1^1/4$″	$5^5/8$″	$8^1/2$″	
1	E	Roof joiner	$3/4$″	$2^3/4$″	$8^1/2$″	
2	F	Roof section	$1/4$″	$5^1/4$″	12″	Tempered Masonite
2	G	Perches	$3/8$″ dia.		$9^1/2$″	Dowel rod
1	H	Hanger rod	$3/16$″ dia.		16″	Minimum length
2	J	Spacer/braces	$1/2$″ dia.		$9^1/2$″	Dowel rod

Hardware

1	$3/16$″ flat washer
1	$1/16$″ cotter key
2	Single-strength glass, $6^5/8$″ × $8^{13}/16$″

7-1 Bird feeder.

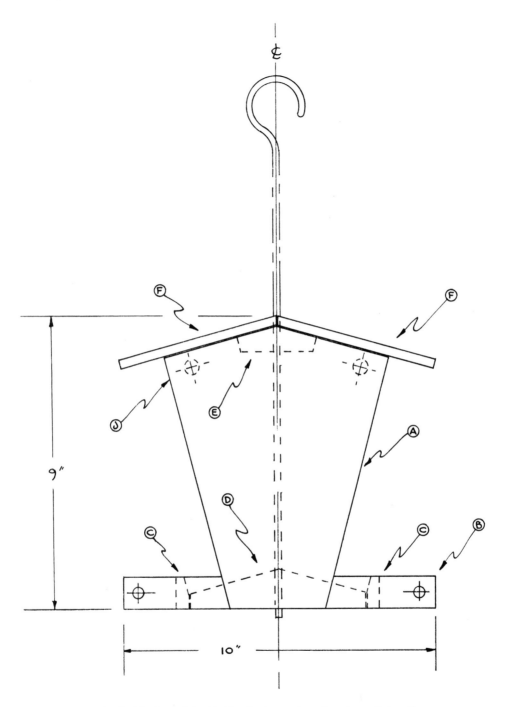

7-2 Study this view of the bird feeder to see how the pieces fit together.

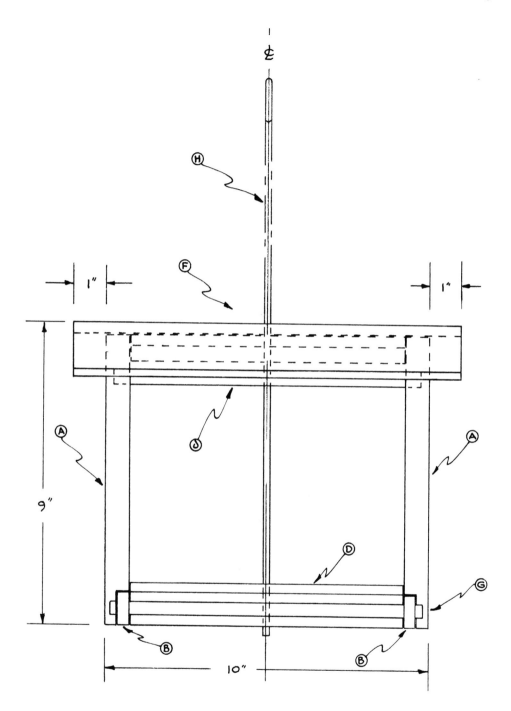

7-3 Become familiar with the component parts and their relationship to each other.

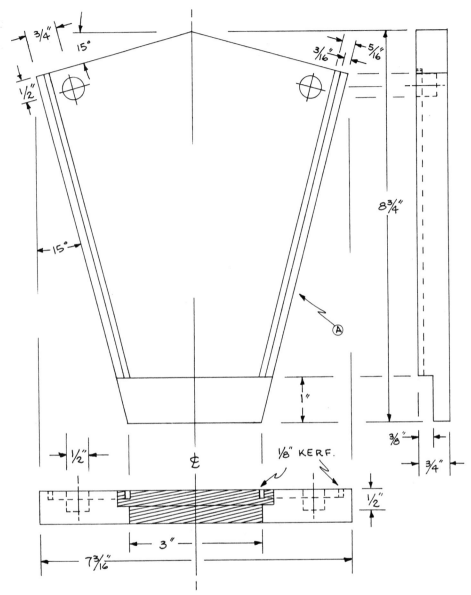

7-4 Cut out the two identical end pieces from 3/4-inch material.

× 8½ inches long. Cut the trough edges (C) from hardwood, ³/8 inch wide × 8½ inches long. While cutting material for the trough edges, go ahead and cut the perch supports pieces (B), 10 inches long, with the same setups. Drill ³/8-inch-diameter holes through each end of each perch support piece (B), through their centerlines and ½ inch from each end. These pieces (B) are now finished except for sanding.

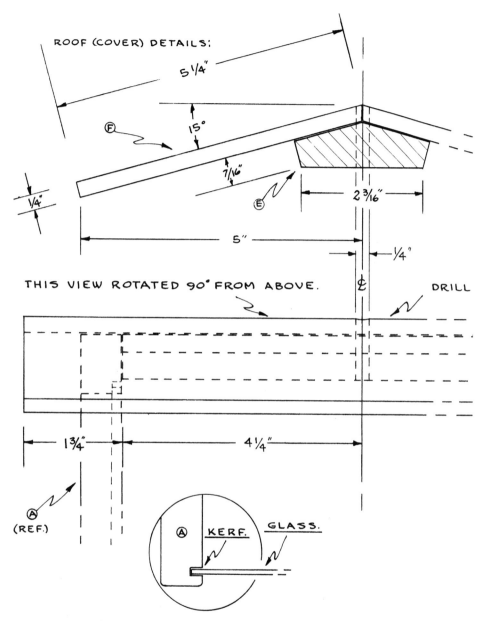

7-5 Note that the two holes, the rabbet cut, and the kerfs are all made on the same inside surface of the end pieces.

Now, tilt the saw blade to 15 degrees and set the rip fence so as to complete roof pieces (F) by beveling one 12-inch edge of each piece only (FIG. 7-5). Reset the rip fence at 1/2 inch from the saw blade and finish cutting the bottom piece (D) as shown. Drill a 3/16-inch hole through the centerline to accommodate the support

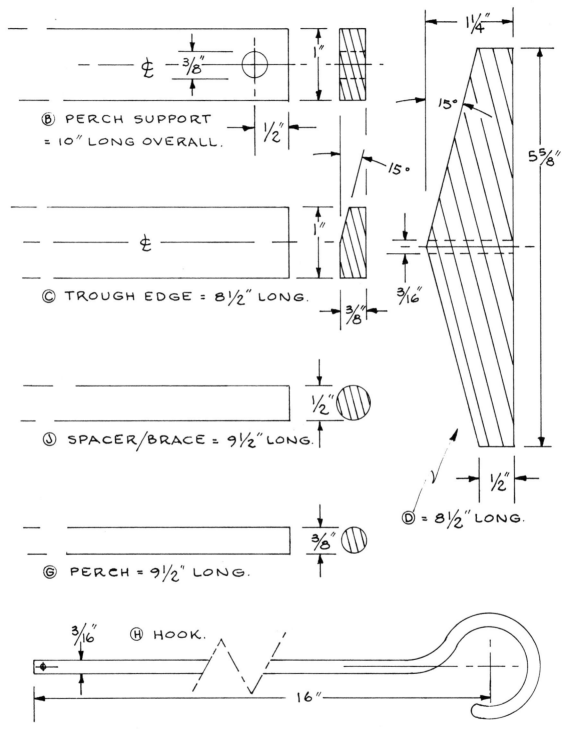

7-6 Note that pieces C, D, E, and F all require 15-degree cuts.

hook (H). Again, reset the rip fence to complete the joiner piece (E), as shown in FIG. 7-5. Squaring off its edges to leave the 2³/16-inch dimension is optional, but do drill the ¹/4-inch-diameter hole through the centerline of the joiner piece.

Set the rip fence to complete the trough edge pieces (C) by beveling one surface only of each piece 15 degrees, and to one-half its width, as shown in FIG. 7-6. Two 9¹/2-inch lengths of ¹/2-inch-diameter dowel rod are required for spacer/brace pieces (J). Two 9¹/2-inch lengths of ³/8-inch diameter dowel rod are required for perches (G).

Sand all these components as appropriate, and you are now ready to start with subassembly.

SUBASSEMBLY

Align the trough edge pieces (C) on either side of bottom piece (D), apply waterproof glue to the mating surfaces, and finish-nail them securely. Align the perch support pieces (B) on each end of the bottom piece (D), apply waterproof glue to the mating surfaces, and secure the pieces (B) with one #18 × 1-inch wire brad at the center for now. Apply glue to the mating surfaces of one end piece (A) and one of the perch pieces just installed. Securely finish-nail through the end piece, the perch support piece, and into the bottom piece. Do this before the glue has set.

Apply a small amount of glue to one end of each spacer/brace rod (J) and press them into the ¹/2-inch diameter holes previously drilled in the end pieces (A). Repeat this procedure with the remaining end piece (A), being careful to "bottom out" the rods (J) into their respective holes. Slip the two perch dowels (G) in place and secure them (FIG. 7-6).

THE ROOF

Align the roof sections (F) along their 15-degree beveled edges while positioning them on the beveled surfaces of the joiner piece (E). Temporarily nail these pieces together so that the finish nail points will have indexed into the roof section joiner no more than about ¹/8 inch deep. Separate the pieces and apply waterproof glue to the mating surfaces of one roof section and its corresponding bevel on piece (E) only. Nail these two pieces together securely.

Next, apply glue to the 15-degree bevels of both roof sections and to the remaining mating surfaces. Finish nailing the roof assembly together. Using the ¹/4-inch hole previously drilled through the roof joiner piece (E) as a guide, drill through the peak of the roof sections to complete the hole for the support hanger piece (H).

THE SUPPORT ROD

Bend an appropriate hook into one end of a length of ³/16-inch diameter rod stock. Drill a ¹/16-inch-diameter hole through its opposite end, approximately ¹/8-inch from the end, as shown in FIG. 7-6. Install rod after painting.

THE GLASS

Cut two pieces of single-strength glass, 8¹³/16 inches × 6⁵/8 inches. Try them for a slip fit within the saw kerfs previously cut into the end pieces (A). Install glasses after painting (FIG. 7-7).

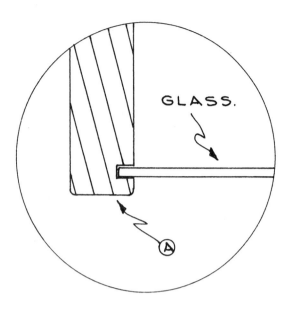

7-7 Try the glass for a slip fit within the saw kerf.

PAINTING

The prototype article was painted with exterior-grade gloss white, except for the roof assembly which was finished in kelly green. The choice of colors is, of course, optional. Three successive coats were applied, lightly sanded between coats. Be careful not to fill the kerfs with paint because you will have to slip the glasses into them.

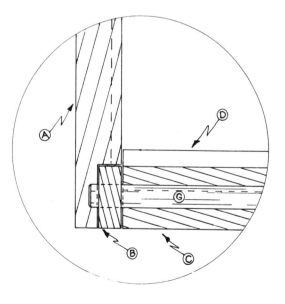

7-8 Slip the glass into place, leaving a clearance at the bottom edges for the feed to pass freely.

FINAL ASSEMBLY

Slip the glass sides into place, leaving a clearance at the bottom edges for the feed to pass freely under (FIGS. 7-7 and 7-8). Maintain the desired clearance by filling the kerfs below the glass with putty or caulking compound.

Pass the drilled end of the hanger rod (H) down through the top of the roof section and through the hole previously drilled through the bottom piece (D). Place a $3/16$-inch flat washer over the end of the rod and slip a $1/16$-inch Cotter key through the hole. The completed feeder is now ready to be filled and put into service.

8
Birdhouse

This novel birdhouse design features a chimney, a supply of firewood, and a nice front porch with a wide, overhanging roof. It also has an easily removable roof section (four screws) to provide access to the interior for house-cleaning between tenants. The floor section is also removable. It, too, is retained in place by four screws (FIG. 8-1).

This birdhouse design is a companion piece to the Bird Feeder, featured in chapter 7.

Birdhouse

Materials List

No. Req.	Part	Name	Thick	Wide	Long	Remarks
1	A	Front end	3/4″	7″	8″	A and B are identical until drilled
1	B	Back end	3/4″	7″	8″	
2	C	Sides	1/4″	4³/4″	8″	Tempered Masonite
1	D	Bottom	3/4″	6³/4″	11″	
1	E	Roof section	1/4″	6″	12″	Tempered Masonite. Identical to E, until comp.
1	F	Roof section	1/4″	6″	12″	
1	G	Chimney	3/4″	1³/4″	9¹/8″	
1	H	Chimney cap	1/4″	7/8″	1¹/8″	
1	J	Perch	1/2″ dia.		3¹/2″	Dowel rod
1	K	Hook support	1″	1¹/2″	2″	
1	L	Hook	3/16″ dia. rod			Length opt.

Hardware

1	3/16″ flat washer
1	1/16″ cotter key
4	#6 × 3/4″ flat-head wood screws
4	#6 × 1¹/2″ flat-head wood screws

8-1 Birdhouse.

INSTRUCTIONS

Read through this chapter completely before beginning construction. Identify the several components represented in FIGS. 8-2 and 8-3. Also, study the Materials List to learn the letter assignments for each piece. This will make the construction phase easier and more enjoyable.

Cut out the two end pieces from ³/₄-inch material as shown in FIGS. 8-4 and 8-5. Corners are rabbeted, left and right, to accommodate the two identical side pieces (C). Cut these pieces from ¹/₄-inch tempered Masonite, 4³/₄ inches × 8 inches, and bevel their edges as shown (FIG. 8-5).

Once you have drilled the ¹/₂-inch-diameter perch hole, and you have cut the entrance hole (diameter as desired) out of one end piece, this part will be identified as the front end (A). Similarly, when you have drilled the three ¹/₂-inch-diameter vent holes through the remaining end piece, it is thus identified as rear end (B).

Apply waterproof glue to the mating surfaces of the sides (C) and the ends (A and B). Finish-nail these components together securely. Cut a 3¹/₂-inch piece of

8-2 Note the various components necessary for the birdhouse.

1/2-inch-diameter dowel rod and turn a spherical radius on one end. This can be accomplished by chucking it in the drill press (not too tightly) and using first a coarse, followed by a finer, sandpaper grit. Chamfer the other end. Now, apply a drop of glue and press the perch piece (J) into its 1/2-inch hole in the end piece (A).

Cut out the floor piece (D) from 3/4-inch material, 63/4 inches wide × 11 inches long, as shown in FIG. 8-6. Set the rip fence on the bench saw at 1/2 inch from the set of the blade. Set the blade for 11/16-inch depth of cut. Hold the bottom of the floor piece against the fence and pass both right and left edges over the blade. Increase the depth of cut to 11/2-inches and pass the back edge over the

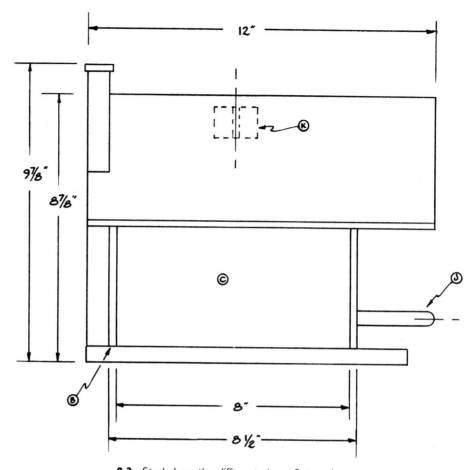

8-3 Study how the different pieces fit together.

blade. Increase the depth of cut to 2¹/₂ inches, and pass the remaining (front) edge over the saw blade.

Next, set the depth of cut for ¹/₄ inch. Set the rip fence for a width of 1¹/₁₆ inches, including the blade. Lay the workpiece upside down on the saw table and, while holding first the right and then the left edges against the fence, pass it over the blade. In like manner, set the fence for a width of 1¹/₂ inches (including the blade) for the back edge of the floor, and at 2¹/₂ inches (including the blade) for the front edge of floor piece (D).

Once these operations have been properly completed there will be a "raised" portion of the floor, ¹/₄-inch × 4⁵/₈ inches × 7 inches. This procedure prevents rain or sprinkler water from getting to the nesting area. If you use a planer blade, the surfaces should require only minimal sanding if any.

Fit the floor (D) to the bottom of the subassembly (A, C, B, C). Locate, drill, and countersink four holes for #6 flat-head wood screws. Drill up through the floor piece so as to engage the ends (A and B).

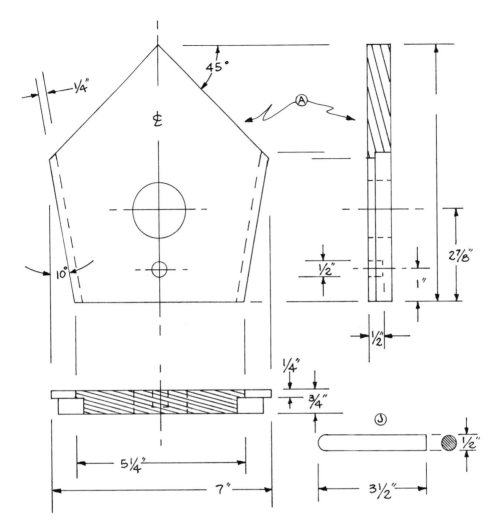

8-4 Cut out the two end pieces from 3/4-inch material.

Cut the chimney piece (G) from 3/4-inch stock as shown in FIG. 8-7. Install its cap (H) with waterproof glue and #18 wire brads. Unless you want to use a contrasting color for the chimney and its cap, go ahead and locate it on the back piece (B) as shown in FIG. 8-7. Glue and finish-nail it in place.

Cut two roof sections from 1/4-inch tempered Masonite, 6 inches × 12 inches. Bevel one 12-inch edge of each piece at 45 degrees. The removable roof section (F) is now done, except for the four retaining screw holes. Locate, drill, and countersink four holes for #6 flat-head wood screws so that they engage the front (A) and back (B) end pieces—and on the right side as viewed from the front. Temporarily install roof section (F).

The remaining roof section (E) differs in that it must be cut out to fit around the chimney (G) as shown in FIGS. 8-7 and 8-8. It also carries the hook support

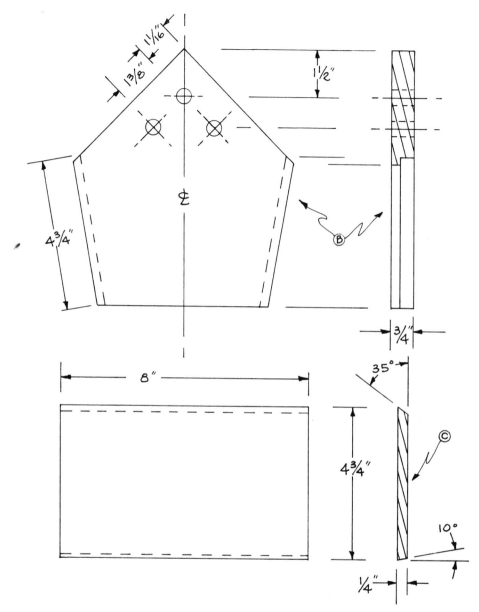

8-5 Notice that the corners are rabbeted left and right to accommodate the two identical side pieces.

block (K). Cut out the block as shown and drill a 3/16-inch diameter hole through it. Permanently glue and nail it in place in the indicated location.

Temporarily install the roof section (E) in place, fitting it to the chimney (G) and snugly against its corresponding bevel on roof section (F). Using the 3/16-inch hole already drilled through block (K) as a pilot hole, drill up through both roof

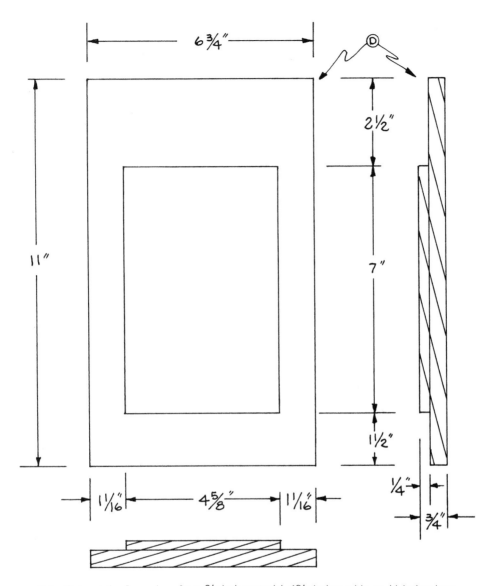

8-6 Cut out the floor piece from 3/4-inch material, 63/4 inches wide × 11 inches long.

sections at their miter to accommodate the support hook (L) (FIG. 8-9). Remove the two roof sections and the fitted floor piece. Sand all the components, if necessary.

Form a hook on one end of a length of 3/16-inch diameter rod stock. Drill a 1/16-inch diameter hole through the rod at about 1/8-inch from the other end.

FINISHING

I recommend that you paint the fitted components separately, prior to final assembly. This affords the best protection and facilitates color separation. You might

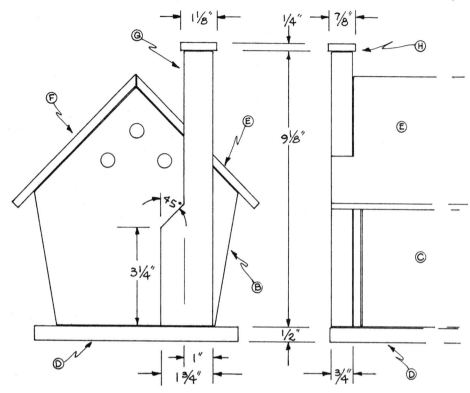

8-7 Cut the chimney piece from ³/₄-inch stock.

want to carry out a particular color scheme at this time. The prototype house was finished in white—floor, ends, sides, perch, chimney, and cap. The roof sections were finished in kelly green (to match the Bird Feeder in chapter 7).

FINAL ASSEMBLY

Secure the roof section (F) in place with four #6 × ³/₄-inch flat-head wood screws. Again, fit the roof section (E) snugly in place (this time permanently) with waterproof glue and finishing nails. Pass the drilled end of the support rod (L) down through the roof sections and the block (K). Slip a ³/₁₆-inch flat washer over the drilled end and secure it in place with a ¹/₁₆-inch cotter key.

Install the painted floor piece (D) in place. Secure it with four #6 × 1¹/₂-inch flat-head wood screws, making sure that the wider "porch" area is in front.

From a dead branch from a tree or shrub cut eight or ten pieces of "firewood," ³/₈ inch to ¹/₂ inch in diameter, and 1¹/₂ inches to 1⁵/₈ inches in length. Stack these on a piece of scrap material, hot gluing them together as the stack builds to the desired proportion. Spray the completed stack with two or three clear finish coats, both as a preservative and to retain the natural color.

When the wood pile has dried, hot glue it on either end of the front porch. The completed house is now ready to be hung in its chosen location, perhaps with a "For Rent" sign displayed.

8-8 Notice that the remaining roof section (E) must be cut out to fit around the chimney.

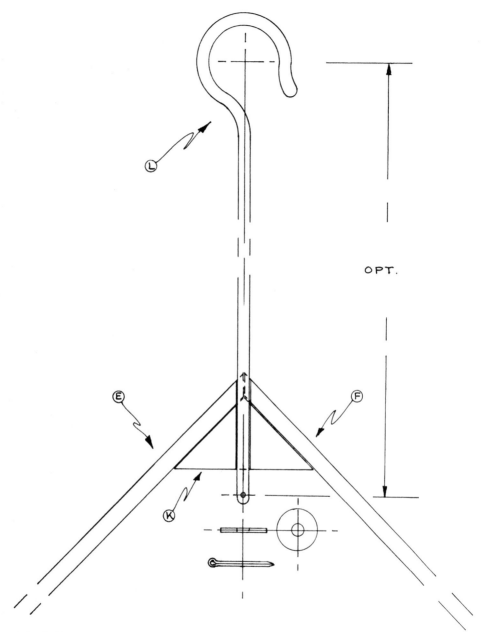

8-9 Drill up through both roof sections at their miter to accommodate the support hook (L).

9

Heart jewelry hanger

This heart design project can be completed in one evening, and it is as useful as it is attractive. It is also an excellent gift item with good commercial potential, as well (FIG. 9-1).

INSTRUCTIONS

If you want to make more than one item, lay out and cut a pattern piece for the basic heart design, following the dimensions shown in FIG. 9-2. Otherwise, lay out the project directly onto a sound piece of 1 × 12 material (3/4-inch × 11 1/4 inches) so that the grain follows the vertical centerline of the heart.

Lay out the centers for the 3/8-inch diameter holes, which are to accommodate the five pegs shown in FIG. 9-3. Bottom-drill these five holes to a depth of only 1/2 inch. Cut out the heart with a band saw or jigsaw. Cut the desired radius around the front surface of the heart with a router or shaper bit. As an alternative, use a hand-sanding block—first with a coarse grit, then with a finer grit to leave a smooth finish.

Heart Jewelry Hanger

Materials List

No. Req.	Part	Description	Thick	Wide	Long	Remarks
1		Heart	3/4″	11 1/4″	11 1/4″	From 1 × 12
5		Pegs	3/8″ dia.		3″	Dowel rod
1		Shelf (optional)	3/4″	3″	6″	

Hardware

1	Screw eye (or other hanging device)
2	Flat-head wood screws, #6 × 1 1/2″ (shelf, optional)

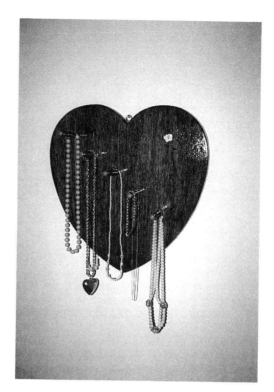

9-1 Heart Jewelry hanger.

THE PEGS

The pegs are to be cut into 3-inch lengths from a $3/8$-inch-diameter dowel rod. Chuck each length into your drill press and sand or rasp them to shape, forming a spherical radius on one end. A half-round rasp will form the reduced diameters shown in FIG. 9-3. Finish up each peg piece with finer grit sandpaper while it is spinning in the chuck. Any indentations made by the chuck jaws will be hidden when the pegs are installed in the heart piece.

THE SHELF

The optional shelf piece shown in FIG. 9-4 can be cut from any $3/4$-inch stock material. Lay out the dimensions as shown, and cut out the shelf, staying just outside the layout lines. Bring it down to dimension with a disk sander and a 1-inch-diameter drum sander. An alternative to the drum sander is to wrap a piece of sandpaper with the desired grit around a short length of 1-inch-diameter dowel rod, using it as a sander block.

Round the edges of its top surface only to conform to the radius previously cut around the perimeter of the heart. If you want to use a cutout in the shelf piece, accomplish this operation now, using a hole saw of the desired diameter. Again, round off the top surface perimeter of the hole and sand the completed component smooth.

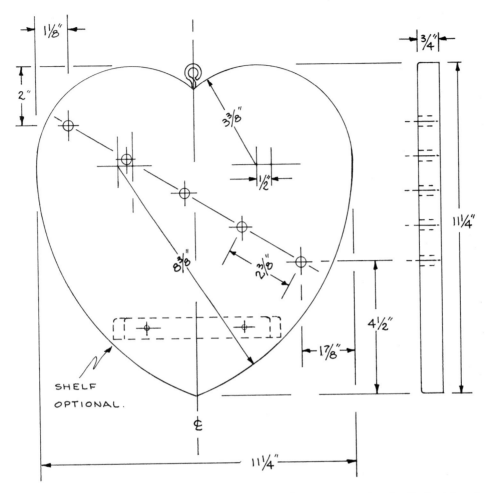

9-2 If you plan to make more than one item, lay out and cut a pattern piece for the basic heart design, following the dimensions.

FINAL ASSEMBLY

Obviously, several final configurations are possible with this basic design, depending upon the intended use of the completed project. A note concerning each is in order here.

Basic heart, with pegs: Sand a slight chamfer on the unfinished ends of five peg pieces. Apply a small amount of glue to these ends and into their corresponding 3/8-inch-diameter mounting holes. Press them into place. As always, be careful not to extrude glue onto the exposed surfaces. This assembly is now ready for final finishing.

Heart, with pegs and shelf: Follow the same procedure, then locate the pilot hole centers for the shelf piece as shown in FIGS. 9-2, 9-3, and 9-4. Install the shelf piece with finish nails or with #6 × 1 1/2 inch wood screws.

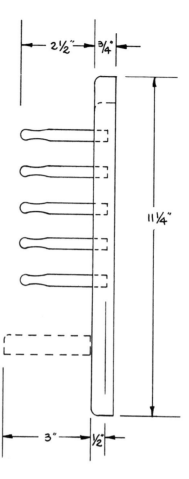

9-3 Lay out the centers for the 3/8-inch-diameter holes, which are to accommodate the five pegs.

Heart with drilled shelf: This configuration may assume two different forms—with peg pieces and without. If you plan to use it with a candle cup or bud vase, you might want to delete the pegs altogether and mount a suitable mirror onto the face of the heart. In this latter instance, the mirror should be installed after final finishing is completed.

FINISHING

You can choose any one of several final finishing procedures for this project. If an attractive grain pattern is evident in the chosen woods, these can be revealed while still maintaining whatever color is to dominate. One prototype project I made was first sprayed lightly with a bright red aerosol enamel. Using a clean, hard-woven cloth and lacquer thinner, I wiped this red coating to reveal the grain of the wood, along with the desired color intensity. Once this coating was thoroughly dry, I added two successive clear coatings, followed with light sandings between coats.

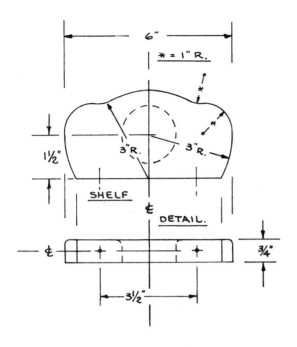

9-4 The optional shelf piece can be cut from any 3/4-inch stock material.

Once finished, all that remains is to install a screw eye or some other hanging device. You can now install a reflective mirror along with a candle cup, bud vase, flower arrangement, etc., if you have chosen this configuration.

The basic project design (heart, with pegs) will also accommodate neckties or belts, as well.

10

Double
heart shelves

This double heart design hanging wall shelf is a bit more difficult to make than some, but it is well worth the extra effort required. A minimal amount of materials is required in its construction, and no special tools are necessary in order for you to turn out a professional looking project (FIG. 10-1).

You can add other embellishments, such as colorful decals, if you want, or you can inscribe names or initials on the two identical heart components upon completion. A variety of self-adhesive plastic letters are available, in a wide range of bright colors, that are perfect for this application.

INSTRUCTIONS

Because the two basic components are the hearts, you should lay out and cut a pattern piece for the hearts first, especially if you plan to make more than one completed assembly. Just follow the dimensions shown in FIG. 10-2. Again, famil-

Double Heart Shelves

Materials List

No. Req.	Part	Name	Thick	Wide	Long	Remarks
2	AB	Hearts	1/2″	83/4″	83/4″	Plywood
1	C	Shelf	3/4″	31/2″	123/4″	
1	D	Shelf	3/4″	3″	6″	
1	E	Peg	3/8″ dia.		3″	Dowel rod
1	F	Brace/peg	3/8″ dia.		39/16″	

Hardware

2	Screw eyes (hangers)
4	#6 × 11/4″ flat-head wood screws (shelves)

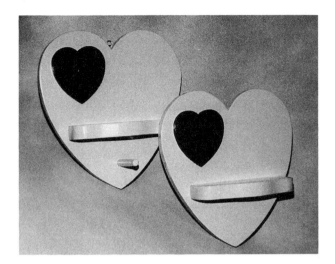

10-1 Double heart shelves.

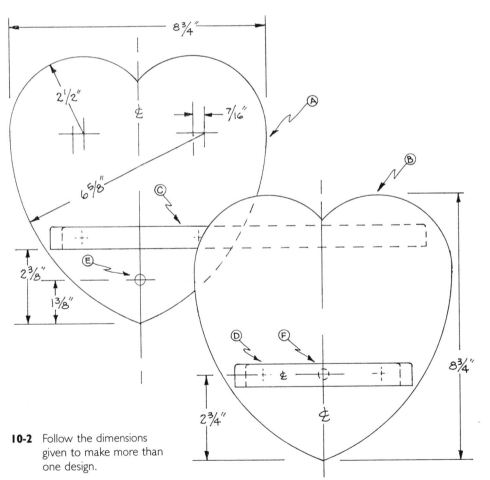

10-2 Follow the dimensions given to make more than one design.

iarize yourself with the Materials List and the letters assigned to each piece so you can follow the instructions more easily.

The only difference in the two hearts is the location of the 3/8-inch diameter hole, so just pilot drill through your pattern piece for both of these holes. The hole for the peg piece (E) will indicate that it is heart A, while the hole for the brace/peg piece (F) makes this heart B (FIG. 10-3).

Cut out these heart pieces from 1/2-inch plywood. Sand their edges smooth, and sand a slight radius around the upper (front) surfaces of both hearts. When drilling the 3/8-inch diameter holes, lay the hearts on a flat piece of scrap 3/4-inch material, securing the hearts to the scrap pieces. This procedure results in a clean hole in both surfaces of the plywood.

THE SHELF PIECES

Lay out the shelf piece (C) on a sound piece of 3/4-inch material and cut it out as shown in FIGS. 10-4, 10-5, and 10-6. Notice that the left end of shelf (C) is cut to the same dimensions as the shelf (D), and that shelf (D) is symmetric about its centerline.

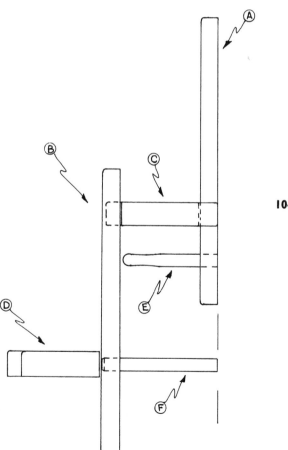

10-3 The hole for the peg piece (E) indicates heart A, while the hole for the brace/leg piece indicates heart B.

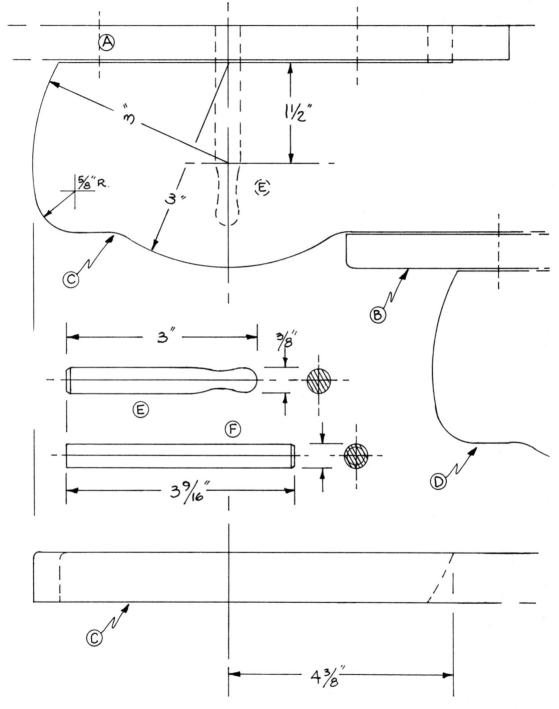

10-4, 10-5 Pattern, double heart shelves.

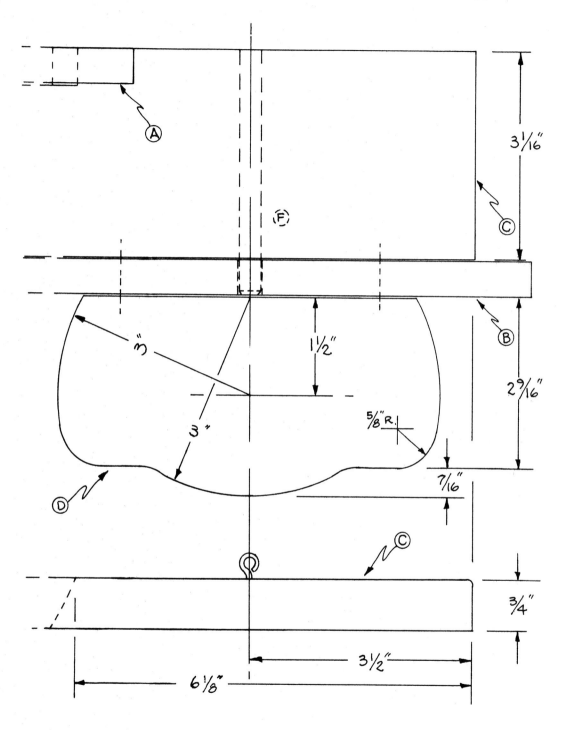

The cutout in the back edge of shelf (C) will be easier to make if the heart piece (A) is aligned with the shelf and its contour is transferred to the shelf, as illustrated in FIG. 10-6.

Sand the edges of these shelves smooth, rounding them slightly around their top surfaces, but only on those curved edges that will be exposed upon final assembly. Notice that the attaching holes for the screws have been indicated for both shelves, and on the hearts as well. Locate and drill these holes through the hearts as marked for the #6 flat-head wood screws. Countersink the holes on the back surface of both heart pieces. Transfer these hole locations to the back edges of each shelf piece and drill pilot holes for the screws, four inches apart, as shown.

THE PEGS

Cut peg pieces (E and F) from 3/8-inch-diameter dowel rod stock, as shown in FIG. 10-4. The reduced diameter on the peg piece (E) can be formed by turning a 3-inch length in your drill press. Chuck this component and use coarse-grit sandpaper wrapped around a short length of one-inch dowel rod to form the desired con-

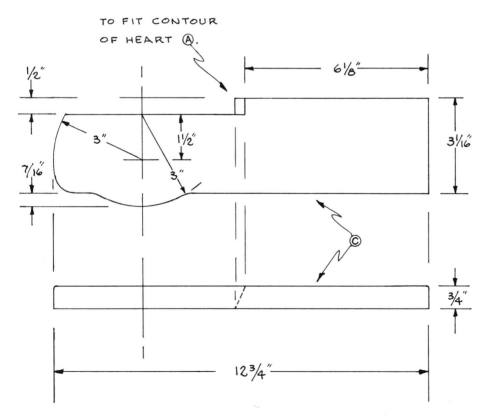

10-6   The cutout in the back of the shelf (C) will be easier to make if the heart piece (A) is aligned with the shelf and its contour is transferred to the shelf.

tour. Finish up with a finer grit for a smooth finish. Sand a slight chamfer on the opposite end of the peg (E), and on both ends of the brace peg (F).

FINAL ASSEMBLY

Align the heart piece (A) in position on the aft edge of the upper shelf piece (C). Apply a small amount of glue to the mating surfaces and secure these parts together with the #6 × 1$1/4$-inch flat-head wood screws.

Align shelf D onto heart piece B and secure them together in like manner. Next, align the subassembly (B−D) onto the front edge of the shelf (C) as shown in FIGS. 10-2 and 10-3. Using small finishing nails, nail through the heart (B) and slightly into shelf (C) only. Check for the accuracy of alignment. Apply a small amount of glue to the mating surfaces, drive in the nails, and set them.

Apply a small amount of glue to the blunt end of the peg (E) and press it into the $3/8$-inch hole in the heart piece (A). Apply glue to the chamfered end of the brace peg (F) and press it into the $3/8$-inch hole in back of the other heart piece (B). This peg serves the dual purpose of a steadying brace (against the wall) and a hanger. Its free end should be in the same plane as the back surface of the heart piece (A).

Install a suitable screw eye in the V of this heart piece (A), at its back surface and at an angle. Once the screw eye is in place, bend it upward so that the eye is in the same plane as the back surface of the heart (A). In like manner, install a similar screw eye in the upper, aft edge of the shelf (C), as shown in FIG. 10-5.

FINISHING

The project is now ready to be finished in your choice of color(s). The prototype project was finished in almond-colored gloss enamel in successive coats. Two small hearts were cut from $1/8$-inch Masonite and finished in bright red enamel. These were centered in the upper, left ''lobes'' of the two heart pieces (A) and (B) for an added touch of color.

11

Stools
or plant stands

This novel set of low stools will delight the youngsters. The set can also serve to show off your specimen pot plants to better advantage. In whichever capacity it is used, it will be sure to attract attention and favorable comment from all who see it in use (FIG. 11-1).

INSTRUCTIONS

Lay out the basic components—heart (H), spade (S), club (C), and diamond (D) designs, as shown in FIGS. 11-2, 11-3, 11-4, and 11-5. If you decide to make more than one set, lay them out on pattern stock. Otherwise, lay out the indicated outlines directly onto some sound $3/4$-inch plywood material.

You can use a band saw to cut out these designs, but I used a hand-held jig-saw. The small radii called for on the spade piece (S) should be accomplished by drilling through at the proper centers with a $3/4$-inch-diameter paddle blade bit, marked $3/8'' R$ on FIG. 11-3. Place the workpiece over a flat piece of scrap material while drilling these holes so that the bit will leave a clean hole when exiting the wood.

Stools or Plant Stands

Materials List

No. Req.	Part	Name	Thick	Wide	Long	Remarks
1	H	Heart (11-2)	$3/4''$	$12''$	$12''$	$3/4''$ plywood
1	S	Spade (11-3)	$3/4''$	$12''$	$12''$	
1	C	Club (11-4)	$3/4''$	$13''$	$12''$	
1	D	Diamond (11-5)	$3/4''$	$13''$	$14''$	
3	A	Doubler (11-6)	$1/4''$	$10''$	$11^{1/2}''$	$1/4''$ plywood
1	B	Doubler (11-7)	$1/4''$	$10^{1/2}''$	$12''$	
13	L	Legs (11-8)	$1^{1/2}''$	$1^{13/16}''$	$6^{1/16}''$	Standard lumber

11-1 Stools or plant stands.

Sand all the edges and surfaces smoothly, leaving a small radius around the perimeter of the front face of each piece.

DOUBLERS

The necessary doublers are made from $1/4$ inch plywood. The same design, FIG. 11-6, is used on three of the tops—heart, spade, and club. The design shown in FIG. 11-7 is for the diamond configuration, only. All are easy to make and only straight cuts are necessary.

The triangular doubler (FIG. 11-6) is an equilateral triangle, $11\ 1/2$ inches on each side. Cut these out on your bench saw. The corner radii can easily be cut as shown with a disk sander, then smooth up the edges and whichever of the surfaces is to be exposed.

The diamond doubler (FIG. 11-7) is also easily cut with straight cuts on the bench saw. Again, smooth its edges and exposed surface. Only one of this configuration is required per set of four pieces.

THE LEGS

Figure 11-8 shows the details of the leg pieces (L). These are to be cut from standard 2-inch ($1\ 1/2$-inch, actually) lumber, and they are triangular in cross-section. Set the saw blade for 30 degrees. Make one pass through the edge of the material (rip cut), and discard the resultant strip thus cut. Set the rip fence at $1\ 13/16$ inches from the saw blade. Turn the material over so that the sharp (60 degree) edge of it

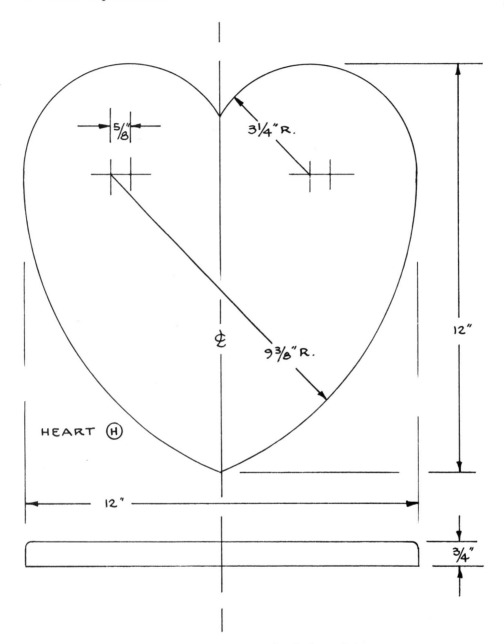

11-2 Basic components for the heart design.

rests against the fence, and pass it through the saw. You now have the desired triangular stock from which to make the individual legs (L). Invert the material after each pass through the saw.

Next, set the blade for a 10-degree cut and cut off the individual legs at 6 inches long. Be sure that these cuts are made so that the ends of the leg pieces are

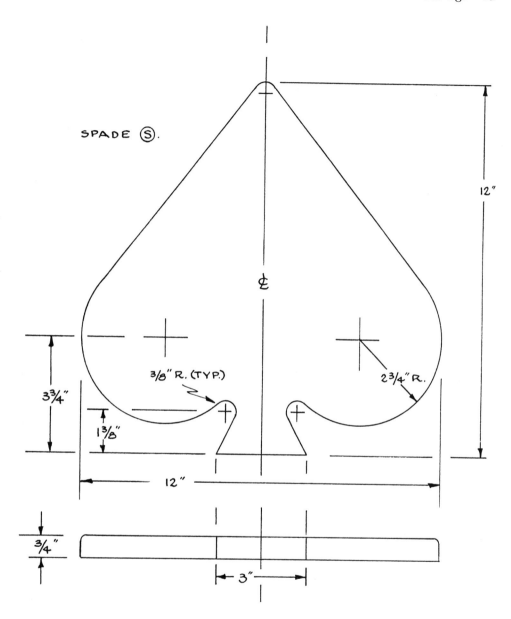

11-3 Basic components for the spade design.

in parallel planes. Thirteen of the legs (L) are required for each set of four stools. The diamond configuration uses four legs, while the other designs use three legs.

Sand the exposed surfaces of the legs on a belt sander. Rotate them carefully on the sander belt when passing from one surface to the next so as to leave a slight radius on each vertex.

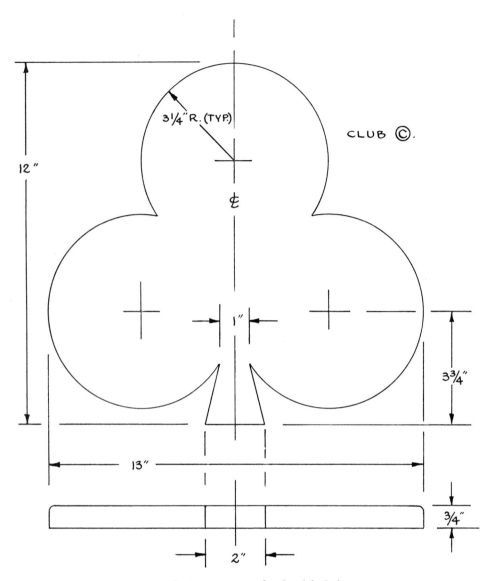

11-4 Basic components for the club design.

FINAL ASSEMBLY

Locate three of the leg pieces (L) on each of three doubler pieces (A), as shown in FIG. 11-6, and on its "best" face. Nail and glue these leg/doubler subassemblies together securely.

Locate four of the leg pieces (L) on the doubler piece (B), as shown in FIG. 11-7. Nail and glue them together in like manner.

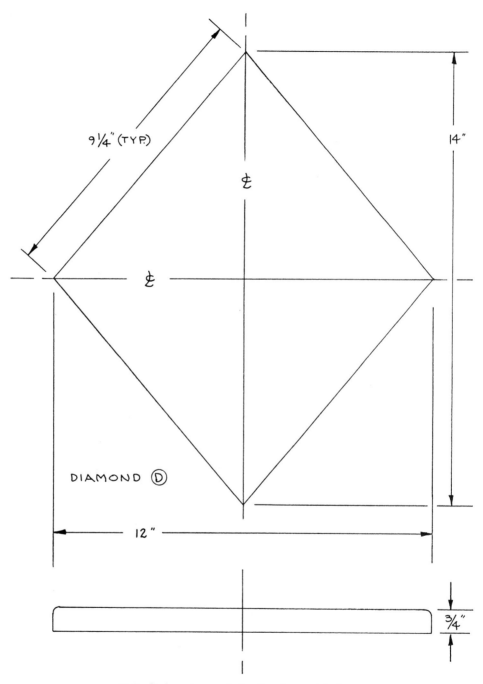

9¼" (TYP.)

14"

℄

℄

DIAMOND Ⓓ

12"

¾"

11-5 Basic components for the diamond design.

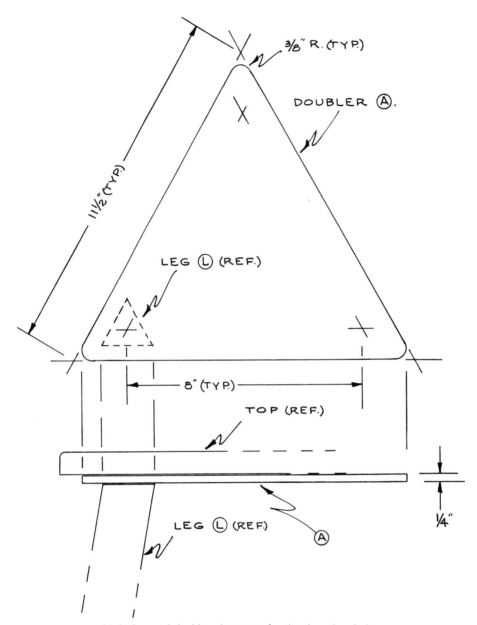

3/8" R. (TYP.)

DOUBLER Ⓐ.

11½" (TYP.)

LEG Ⓛ (REF.)

8" (TYP.)

TOP (REF.)

LEG Ⓛ (REF.)

Ⓐ

¼"

11-6 Leg and doubler placement for the three-leg designs.

Align these leg subassemblies on the underneath sides of their appropriate top pieces—(H), (S), (C), and (D)—as shown in FIGS. 11-6 and 11-7. Apply wood glue to the mating surfaces, and nail or screw them together securely from the underneath sides.

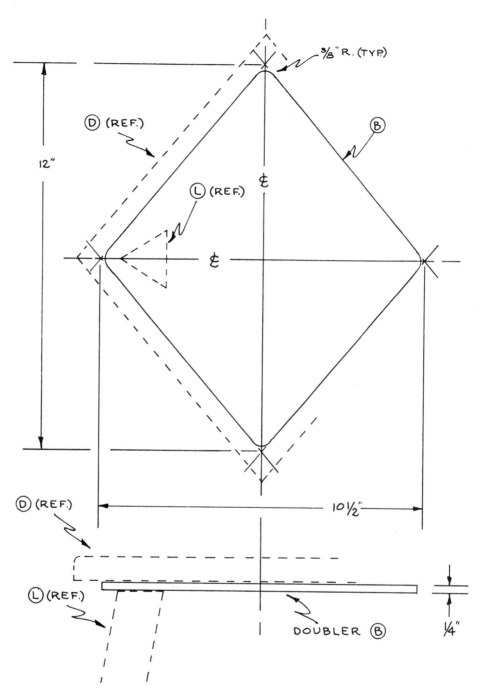

II-7 Leg placement for the four-leg design (diamond pattern only).

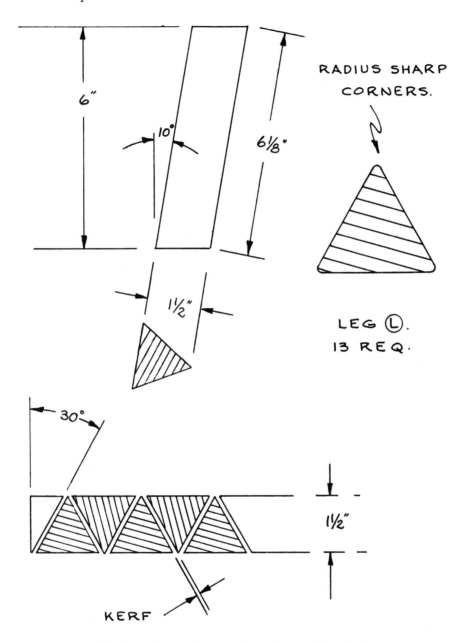

RADIUS SHARP
CORNERS.

LEG Ⓛ.
13 REQ.

11-8 Leg pieces are to be cut from standard 2-inch lumber.

FINISHING

If the material you chose for this project has a particularly attractive grain pattern, you might wish to let it show through the color coat. If so, spray the exposed surfaces of both the heart piece (H) and the diamond piece (D) with red enamel. While the surfaces are still wet, start wiping them with a lint-free cloth or sponge material, wetted with lacquer thinner. When you get the right clarity of grain pattern and color intensity, lay these pieces aside to dry.

Follow the same procedure with the club (C) and spade (S)—using black enamel this time, of course. When you follow this up with a clear coat, your plant stands or stools are ready for show—or service.

12

Heart candle sconces

These matching candle sconces require very little materials and can be completed in comparatively little time (FIG. 12-1). They are really an attractive project and nice to display and use. They are also a novel gift item with excellent commercial potential.

Most woodworkers' shops already have enough scrap materials around to make at least a pair or so, as you will notice from a study of the Materials List and FIGS. 12-2, 12-3, and 12-4. If you choose a hardwood or another wood with an attractive grain pattern, you might want to finish the completed project with an appropriate stain, followed by a clear final finish.

INSTRUCTIONS

Lay out the pattern for the heart piece (B) on heavy paper or cardboard, following the dimensions shown in FIG. 12-4—or directly onto the chosen material if you plan to make only one pair.

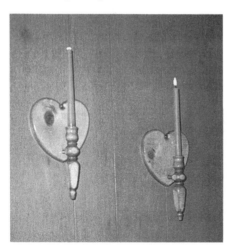

12-1   Heart candle sconces.

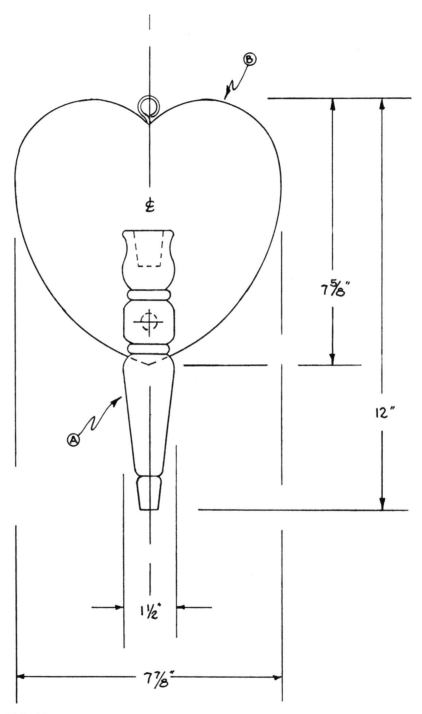

12-2 You can make these heart sconces from scrap pieces found around your shop.

Heart Candle Sconces

Materials List

No. Req.	Part	Name	Thick	Wide	Long	Remarks
1	A	Candlestick	1¹/₂"	1¹/₂"	8"	For one unit
1	B	Heart	³/₄"	7⁷/₈"	7⁵/₈"	For one unit
1	C	Support	¹/₂" dia.		3"	Dowel rod

Hardware

1		Screw eye (or other hanging device)

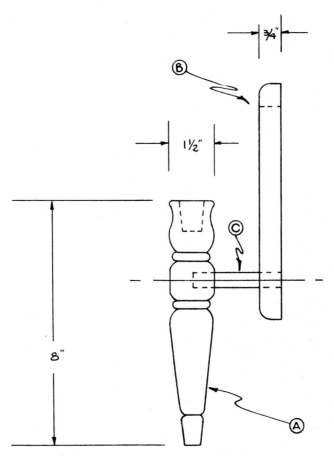

2-3 The hole indicated accommodates one end of the support piece.

This enchanting rocking horse, made from birch plywood and oak, is rugged enough to meet the demands of even the most energetic cowpokes.

Perfect for any easy weekend project, these chicken bookends invite many possible finish variations.

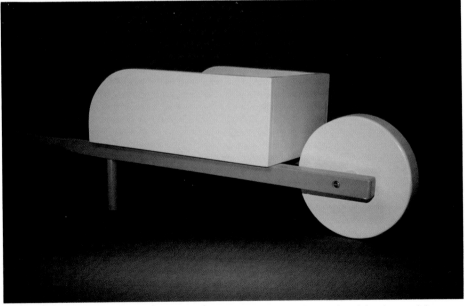

An attractive wheelbarrow is easy to construct and requires only minimal materials.

This sturdy swing seat will accommodate all children, from tiny tots to those of school age.

Plant stands (or children's stools) are sure to be welcome gifts or conversation pieces.

This handsome goose candy dispenser is ready to hold your favorite sweets.

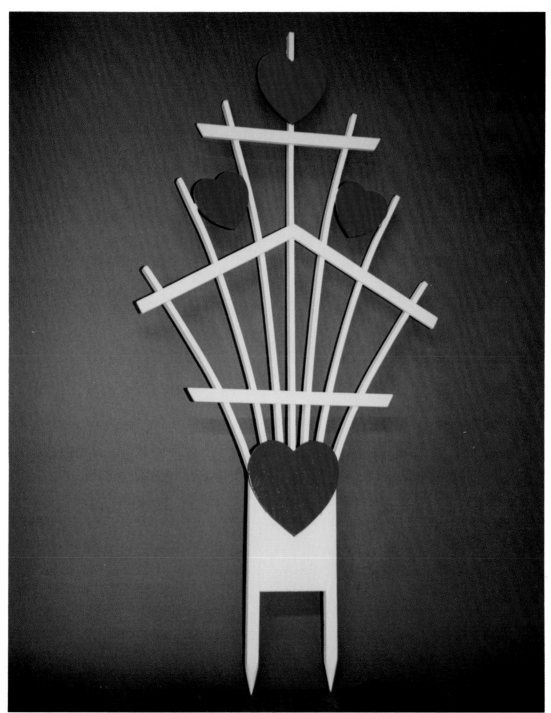

Designed for use in larger pots or planters, this practical and attractive trellis will brighten anyone's garden, indoors or out.

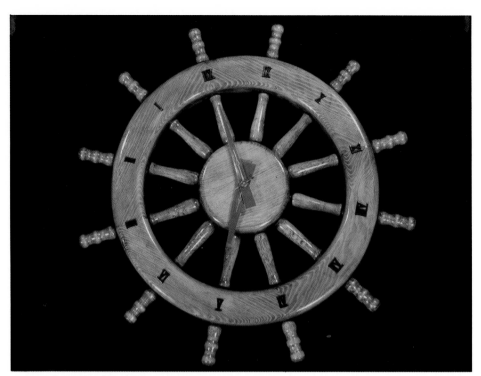

For those with a nautical leaning, a helmsman's clock is the ideal gift.

Feathered friends will look forward to returning from their hectic days of worm-catching if they have an inviting home like this one.

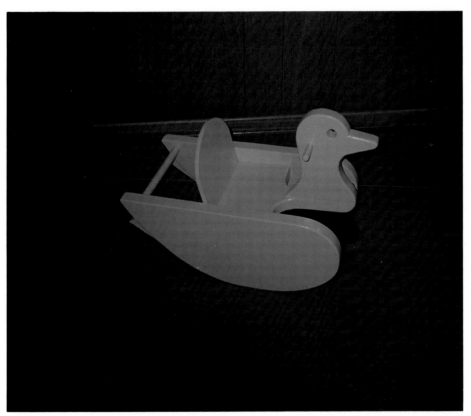

"Rocky Duck" is a sturdy, inexpensive, and easy-to-make riding toy that is sure to delight the preschool set.

A ball gum dispenser that works every time—and without a coin!—will be a definite hit with the youngsters.

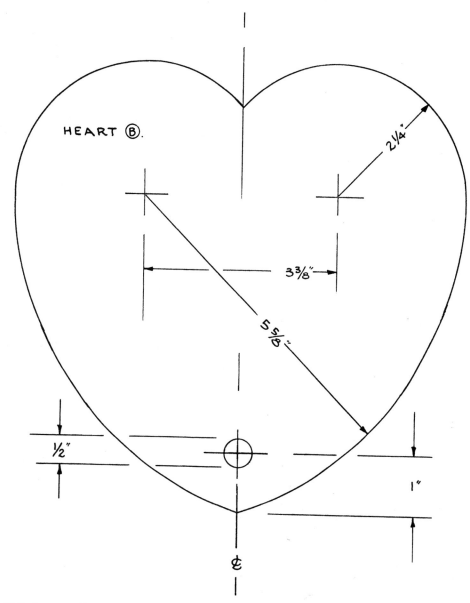

HEART Ⓑ.

2¼"

3⅜"

5⅝"

½"

1"

₵

12-4 Lay out this pattern for the heart pieces (B) on heavy paper or cardboard, following the dimensions shown.

Conventional ³/₄-inch shelf pine was used in the prototype pair, with a few tight knots and a pretty grain pattern. The Early American stain, followed by clear finish coatings, resulted in a superior looking completed project.

Cut two (or more) of the heart components and sand the edges and exposed surfaces smooth. Sand a slight radius around the perimeter of the front surfaces.

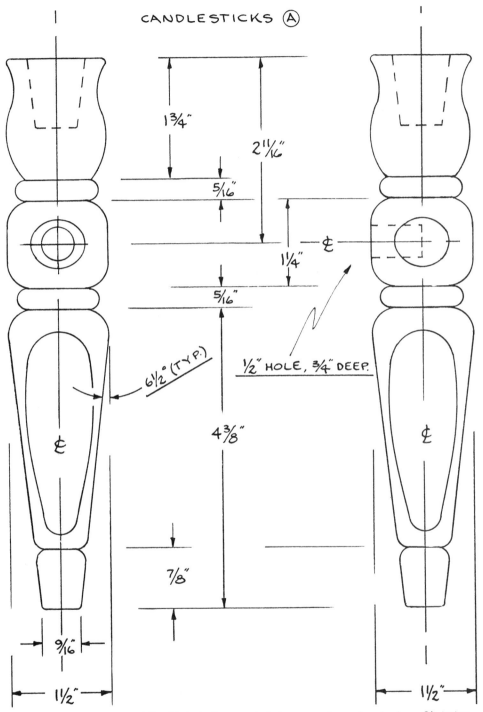

CANDLESTICKS Ⓐ

1¾"

2¹¹⁄₁₆"

5⁄₁₆"

1¼"

5⁄₁₆"

¢

6½° (TYP.)

½" HOLE, ¾" DEEP.

4⅜"

¢

7⁄₈"

9⁄₁₆"

1½"

1½"

12-5 Locate and bottom-drill a ¹/2-inch-diameter hole in one surface of each piece, ³/4 inches deep and at 2¹¹/16 inches from the cup end.

Locate and drill the 1/2-inch diameter hole through, as shown. Place a flat piece of scrap material underneath the workpiece to prevent possible splitting out as the drill bit exits the heart piece. This done, these parts are now ready for final finishing or final assembly.

THE CANDLESTICKS

The candlestick components (A) are turned from 1$\frac{1}{2}$-inch × 1$\frac{1}{2}$-inch × 8-inch stock, which can be ripped from almost any 2-inch (actually 1$\frac{1}{2}$-inch) material desired. Before centering them in the lathe, be sure to cut the 6$\frac{1}{2}$-degree bevels in all four surfaces as shown in FIG. 12-5.

Locate and bottom drill a 1/2-inch diameter hole in one surface of each piece, 3/4-inch deep and at 2$\frac{11}{16}$ inches from the cup end, as shown in FIG. 12-5. This

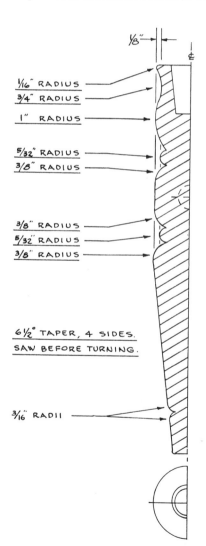

12-6 Center these pieces in the lathe and follow the dimensions shown.

1/8"

1/16" RADIUS
3/4" RADIUS
1" RADIUS
5/32" RADIUS
3/8" RADIUS
3/8" RADIUS
5/32" RADIUS
3/8" RADIUS

6½° TAPER, 4 SIDES.
SAW BEFORE TURNING.

3/16" RADII

hole is to accommodate one end of the support piece (C) (FIG. 12-3). The candle cups in the top ends of these pieces are to be formed after turning and sanding has been accomplished.

Center these pieces in the lathe and follow the dimensions shown in FIGS. 12-5 and 12-6. Once the indicated contours have been cut as shown (or as desired), sand these pieces while they are still turning. Depending on the hardness of the wood chosen, you might want to sand first with a coarser grit, then with a finer finishing grit to achieve a smooth, professional surface.

Drill into the top center of each piece with a 5/8-inch-diameter drill bit to a depth of no more than 1 inch, following the centerlines of the pieces (A). The taper may be established by using a short length of 1/2-inch-diameter dowel rod, wrapped with sandpaper and chucked in your drill press. While holding each piece at a slight angle to the rotating sander thus formed, turn it gently and steadily until the hole is properly tapered to receive the candle.

The support piece (C) is made from a piece of 1/2-inch-diameter dowel rod, 3 inches long. Sand a slight chamfer on both ends of each piece.

FINAL ASSEMBLY

If you decide to use a stain, you might want to apply it to all three components before assembling them.

Apply wood glue to one end of a support piece (C) and press it into the 1/2-inch-diameter hole previously drilled through heart piece (B), so that it is flush with the back surface of the heart.

Apply glue to the opposite end of part (C) and press it into the hole previously drilled into the candlestick piece (A) so that it bottoms out. Be sure that the vertical centerlines of both pieces (A and B) are in the same plane.

FINISHING

If the complete project has been stained, it can now be sprayed with successive clear coatings. If you choose to use a color or colors, apply a sealer coat before making the final color applications. In any event, you'll obtain a better final finish if you lightly sand between the final coatings. Allow each successive coat to dry thoroughly before applying the next.

All that remains is to install a screw eye (or other hanging device), and your heart candle sconces are ready to be displayed and admired.

The overall appearance may be enhanced by the use of decals, striping, small mirrors, etc.—and, of course, a pair of attractive tapers.

13
Child's chair

This sturdy little chair will be a delight to preschoolers. It is easy to make and inexpensive, as well. Also, it is easy to cut five (5) from a single sheet of 1/2-inch-thick plywood (FIGS. 13-1 and 13-2).

These are also excellent gift pieces, especially if you personalize them with a name or initial cut from 1/8-inch Masonite and finished in a bright, contrasting color. Such initials or designs can be glued to the sides (D), or a single one could be affixed to the back piece (B).

INSTRUCTIONS

If you decide to make a single chair, cut it from a piece of material 30 inches wide by 32 inches long (FIG. 13-2). However, you might at least consider ripping up a full sheet, as indicated, while the bench saw is set up.

Child's Chair

Materials List

No. Req.	Part	Name	Thick	Wide	Long	Remarks
2	A	Rocker *	3/4″	1″	18″	Hardwood
1	B	Back	1/2″	12 1/2″	14″	1/2″ plywood
2	C	Cleat	3/4″	3/4″	7 1/2″	Rip from scrap
2	C	Cleat	3/4″	3/4″	11″	
2	D	Side	1/2″	14″	17 1/2″	1/2″ plywood
1	S	Seat	1/2″	11 5/16″	14″	
2	E	Heart **	1/8″	4″	4″	Masonite

Hardware

8	#6 × 1″ flat-head wood screws (Seats & backs)
8 *	#6 × 1″ flat-head wood screws (Optional rockers)
8	#6 chrome dimpled washers (Seats & backs)

* Rockers A are optional
** Hearts (or other decorative pieces for sides) are optional

13-1   Child's chair.

Note that the cuts have been numbered so they require only four setups. The figure assumes that a plywood blade is being used and that the kerf will be approximately .10 inch.

Referring to FIG. 13-2, first set the rip fence for a 14-inch cut and make the six cuts as indicated. Once this is done, reset the fence for $12^{1}/2$ inches, and cut out five back pieces (B). Next, set the fence for $11^{5}/16$ inches to cut five seat pieces (S). Finally, make the $17^{1}/2$-inch cuts to form the ten side pieces (D).

The $3^{1}/2$-inch radius, semicircular cutout in the side pieces (D) is the same as that in the back pieces (B)—with one exception. Notice that the center for this cutout on the back piece is located $1/2$ inch from the 14-inch edge (FIG. 13-5). It should be possible to stack two or more of these pieces at a time to save considerable time and effort in cutting them out.

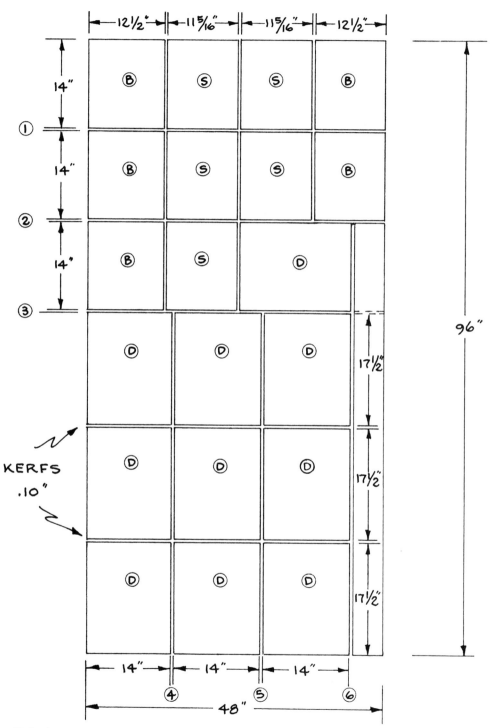

13-2 As many as five of these projects can be cut from a single sheet of 1/2-inch thick plywood.

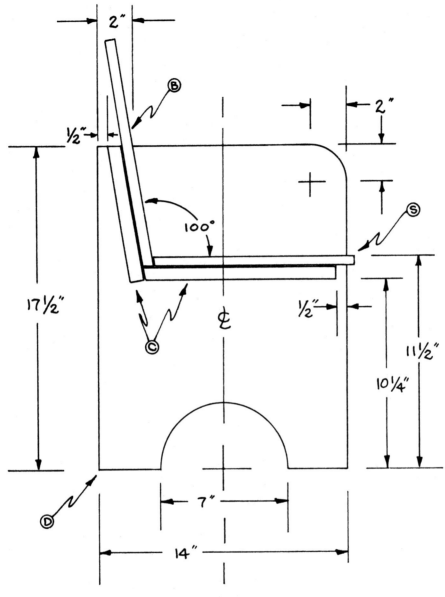

L.H. SHOWN, R.H. OPPOSITE.

13-3 Notice the location of the cleat pieces (C) and the side pieces (D).

Round the two top corners of the back pieces (B) at one inch, and one upper corner of the side pieces (D) on a two-inch radius (FIG. 13-4).

Set the saw blade to 10 degrees tilt and make the cuts required on the lower 14-inch edge of the backs (B), and on one 14-inch edge of the seat pieces (S), as shown in FIG. 13-5. All the primary components are now ready for finally sanding

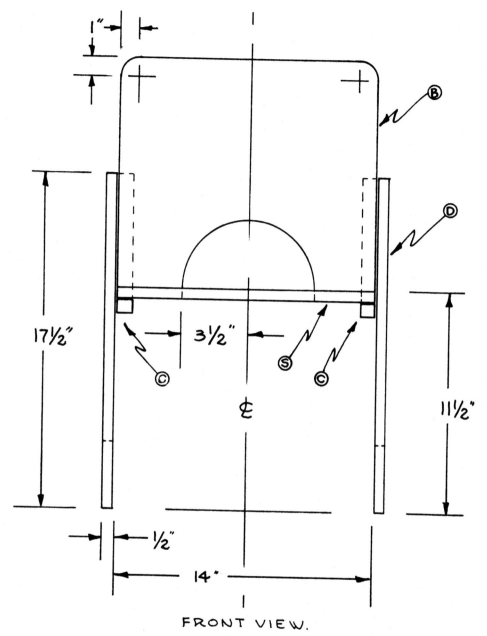

1"

17½"

3½"

11½"

½"

14"

℄

B

D

S

C

C

FRONT VIEW.

13-4 Round the two top corners of the back pieces (B) at 1 inch and one upper corner of the side pieces (D) on a 2-inch radius.

as necessary. Fill any voids that may have appeared in the plywood edges prior to final finishing.

The final pieces to be cut are the cleats which support the seats ($^3/_4$-inch × $^3/_4$-inch × 11 inches, two required) and those for the backs ($^3/_4$ × $^3/_4$ × 7$^1/_2$

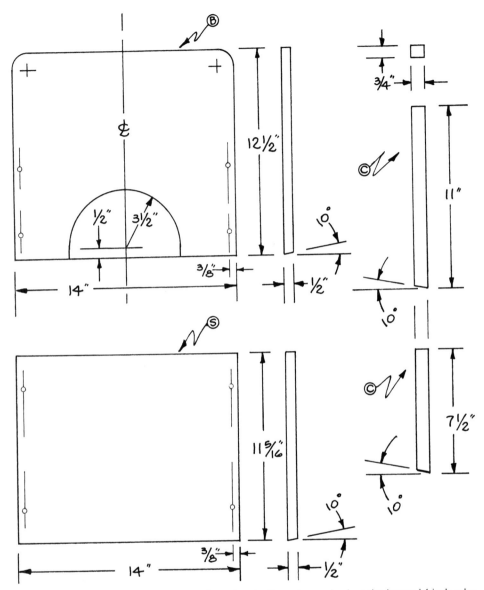

13-5 Set the saw blade to 10 degrees tilt and make the cuts required on the lower 14-inch edge of backs (B), and on one 14-inch edge of seat pieces (S).

inches, two required). They can be ripped from almost any available scrap material and should be beveled at 10 degrees on one end only, as shown in FIG. 13-5.

SUBASSEMBLY

Lay out the locations for the cleat pieces (C) on the inside surfaces of side pieces (D), as shown in FIGS. 13-3, 13-4, and 13-6. Choose the better surfaces for outside

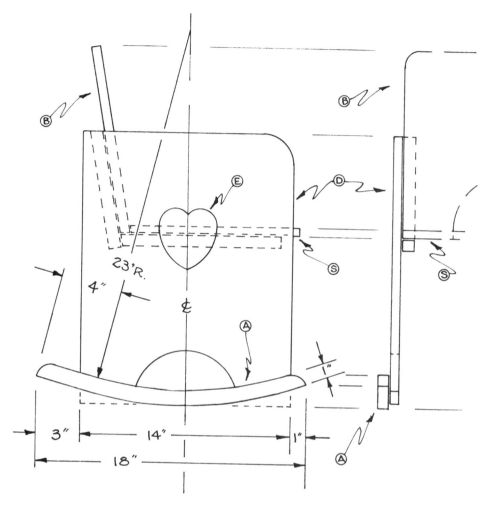

13-6 Cut a heart design approximately 4 × 4 inches from 1/8-inch Masonite.

exposure, of course. Glue and either finish-nail or wood-screw the cleats securely in place, remembering that one right-hand and one left-hand configuration are required per chair.

FINISHING

The prototype chair was sanded, sealed, and finished in gloss enamel, almond color, lightly sanded between coats. A heart design was cut from 1/8-inch Masonite, approximately 4 inches × 4 inches, as shown in FIG. 13-6. The hearts were finished on one side in bright red gloss enamel and mounted on the two side pieces (D) with glue and #18 × 1/2-inch wire brads. A cotton swab makes a good touch-up brush for the tiny nail heads, to render them inconspicuous.

You might want to match some existing color scheme, of course, if you know where the chair(s) will be placed. If the wood exhibits a nice grain pattern, you

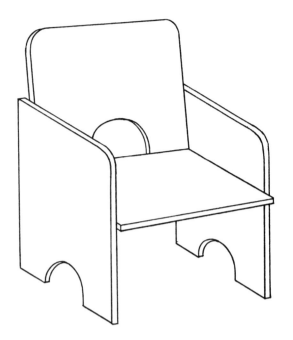

13-7 Assembled Child's Chair.

might prefer to use a stain or tint, followed by successive clear coats.

After the final finishing has been applied, it is time to locate and drill the holes for the #6 × 1-inch wood screws in the back pieces (B) and in the seat pieces (S) as shown in FIG. 13-5. Locate these holes in the opposite edges of both seat and back pieces 3/8 of an inch from, and in a parallel line with, the edges as indicated.

FINAL ASSEMBLY

Preliminarily fit the pre-drilled seat and back pieces into place between a matching pair of side pieces, starting with the back. Using a sharp punch or an awl, reach through the screw holes and pierce the cleats sufficiently to mark the hole locations.

If hardwood has been used for the cleats, it might be necessary to drill pilot holes into them to receive the attaching screws. Use a small extension drill bit, being careful not to allow the drill chuck to come into contact with the finished side pieces. A length of stiff wire, cut off with diagonal cutting pliers, will suffice for a fairly good extension bit.

Reassemble the chair components and install the wood screws, using a dimpled finishing washer under the head of each screw (FIG. 13-7).

THE ROCKING CHAIR

Cut out two rockers (A) as shown in FIG. 13-6 from a good hardwood. Clamp them together and bring their outside radii into conformity with a belt sander. Locate the completed rockers onto two pieces (D) as indicated, and clamp them into place. Drill holes for the #6 attaching screws through sides (D) from the inside, and countersink them.

Mark and saw off that portion of each side extending below the rockers (indicated by broken lines). Sand these edges smooth. All that remains is to apply wood glue to the mating surfaces and reinstall the rockers, securing them in place with the #6 × 1-inch flat head wood screws.

FINISHING TOUCHES

There are any number of decalcomania designs available in a variety of colors, which can enhance the appearance of your completed chairs.

A scrap of good carpeting in matching or tastefully contrasting color(s) can be fitted to the seat over double-stick tape. Cut it 14 inches wide by about 13 inches so as to have a net fit from side to side and enough to roll over the front edge of the seat. Staple it in place, making sure the staples are recessed into the carpet pile.

If you want to use tailored chair covers, consider using snap fasteners to retain them in place. Such fasteners also make it easier to remove the covers for cleaning or replacing.

14
Child's
swing seat

This swing seat is very sturdy and is easy to make. It will accommodate children from tiny tots to those of primary school age. A leather or webbing belt fitted with a buckle should be provided for the littlest "swingers" as a safety measure.

Many of the component parts can be cut from the scrap materials that always seem to accumulate around almost every woodworking shop. Six of the parts required for this project have a $1^1/2$-inch dimension, with one of them being $1^1/2$ inches × $1^1/2$ inches in cross section. Since standard two-inch lumber is actually $1^1/2$ inches thick, you can get many pieces rather easily by planning the cuts to be made at each setup. The prototype swing design shown in FIG. 14-1 was cut from a three-foot length of standard 2 × 4, except for the arm pieces. These were cut from two feet of 1 × 4 (and 1 × 3 would have sufficed).

INSTRUCTIONS

Study carefully the Materials List and coordinate this information with FIGS. 14-2 and 14-3. Inventory your available materials before buying new stock. Before setting up the bench saw for the first cuts, it might be helpful to know the total lengths required of each width and thickness for one complete project. (See Length Table.)

Once the material has been cut to the indicated sizes and in sufficient quantity, cut it into proper lengths as shown in (FIGS. 14-2 through 14-6). If you use a planer blade, it will greatly minimize the sanding necessary later. Some of the parts require two or more additional operations, as you will see. Whether you are building one or several of these swings, accomplish all operations that require the same setup before breaking down that setup.

If you are building only one swing, you can just lay out the angles, hole locations, etc., directly onto the pieces just cut off. If several are to be built, or if more are contemplated at a later date, keep one complete set of finished components—along with any setup notes, jigs, etc.

Notice that completed parts A and C must be right-hand and left-hand, and that one of each is required per swing. Parts B, D, E, and F are either right or left and thus interchangeable.

Child's Swing Seat

Materials List

No. Req.	Part	Name	Thick	Wide	Long	Remarks
2	A	Arm rest	$3/4''$	$2''$	$12''$	Cut two from 1 × 4 × 24".
2	B	Back support	$3/4''$	$1^1/2''$	$14''$	All of these parts can be ripped from 2 × ? scrap.
2	C	Seat support	$1''$	$1^1/2''$	$11^3/8''$	
2	D	Arm support	$1^1/2''$	$1^1/2''$	$5^1/5''$	
6	E	Seat slats	$5/16''$	$1^1/2''$	$16''$	
5	F	Back slats	$5/16''$	$1^1/2''$	$8^5/8''$	
2	G	Back slat retainers	$1''$	$1^1/2''$	$12^1/2''$	

Hardware

4	$3/16'' \times 2^1/2''$ flat-head wood screws
2	$1/4'' \times 1^1/2''$ eye bolt
2	$3/16'' \times 2^1/4''$ round-head machine screws
2	$1/4'' \times 3''$ screw eyes
2	$1/4'' \times 2''$ carriage bolts
2	$1/4'' \times 2^1/4''$ carriage bolts
4	$3/16''$ flat washers
8	$1/4''$ flat washers
2	$3/16''$ nuts
10	$1/4''$ nuts
	Chain or rope as required
	Leather or web belt

14-1 Child's swing seat.

Length of Parts

Dimensions	Linear feet per swing	For part
5/16" × 11/2"	12	Slats E and F
3/4" × 11/2"	21/2	Back supports B
3/4" × 2"	2	Arms A
1" × 11/2"	4	C and G
11/2" × 11/2"	1	Arm supports D

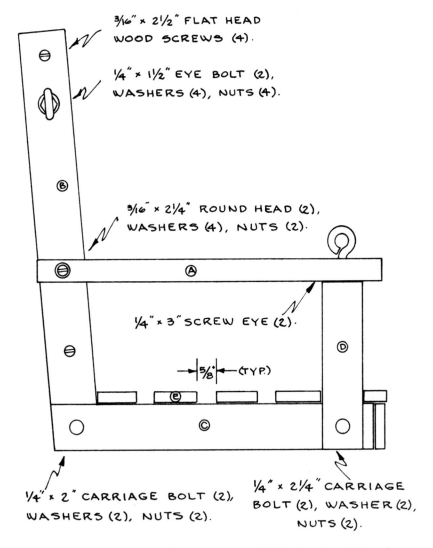

3/16" × 21/2" FLAT HEAD WOOD SCREWS (4).

1/4" × 11/2" EYE BOLT (2), WASHERS (4), NUTS (4).

3/16" × 21/4" ROUND HEAD (2), WASHERS (4), NUTS (2).

1/4" × 3" SCREW EYE (2).

5/8 (TYP.)

1/4" × 2" CARRIAGE BOLT (2), WASHERS (2), NUTS (2).

1/4" × 21/4" CARRIAGE BOLT (2), WASHER (2), NUTS (2).

14-2 Make up two side subassemblies, one right-hand and one left-hand.

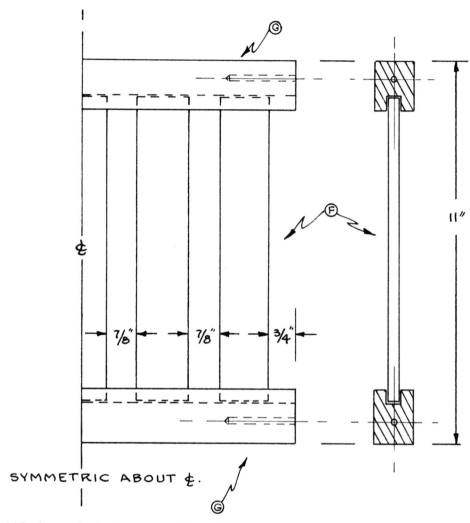

14-3 Arrange five back slat pieces (F) in parallel between the two back slat retainer pieces (G) so that their ends are fully fitted.

SIDE SUBASSEMBLY

Make up two side subassemblies, one right-hand and one left-hand, as shown in FIG. 14-2. Countersink the two 3/16-inch-diameter holes on the outside surfaces only of the back support parts (B). These holes are to accommodate the screws which will attach the back subassembly later.

If the swing is to be clear-coated with varnish, these components can now be assembled with the hardware. If the swing is to be color-coated, it should only be fitted temporarily, then assembled after final finishing. Mark the parts so assembled, or run a piece of string through their holes, to identify them as a fitted set.

Start by installing a back support part (B) and an arm support part (D) onto a seat support part (C) with 1/4-inch carriage bolts, washers, and nuts. Fit the appro-

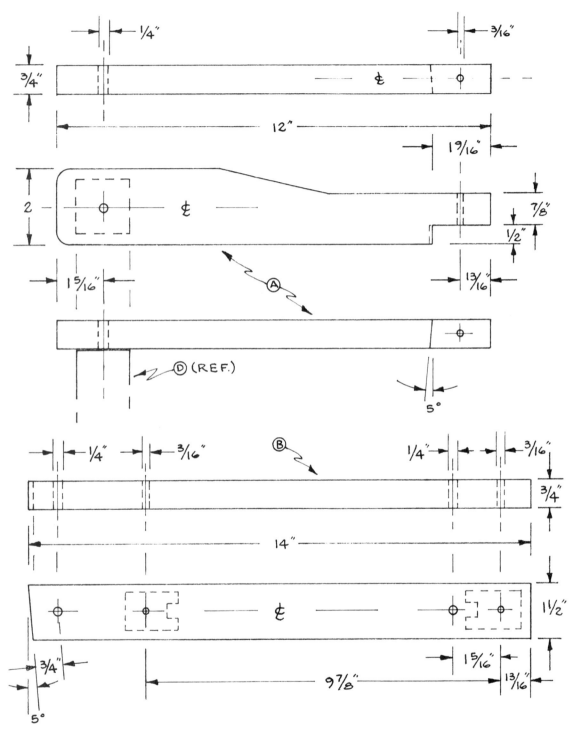

14-4 Note the dimensions of the arm pieces (A) and the back support piece (B).

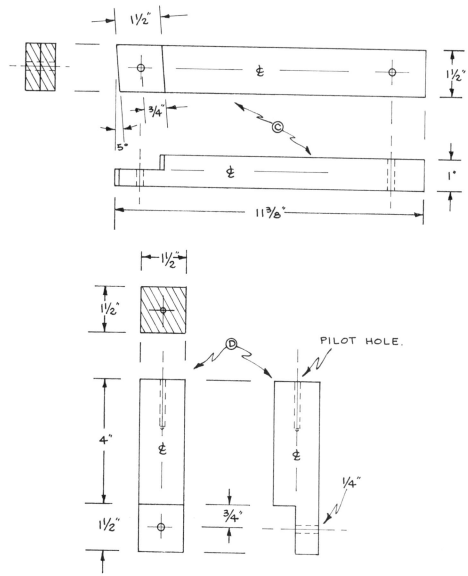

14-5 Note how the pieces fit together to form the side subassembly.

priate arm piece (A) in place. Attach its aft end to the back support piece (B) (FIG. 14-4). Align the 1/4-inch hole in the arm piece with the pilot hole previously drilled in the top center of the arm piece (D). Finish-nail the arm to its support piece and install the 1/4-inch screw eye in place.

THE BACK SUBASSEMBLY

Arrange five back slat pieces (F) in parallel between two back slat retainer pieces (G) so that their ends are fully fitted into the 5/16-inch × 5/16-inch dado grooves.

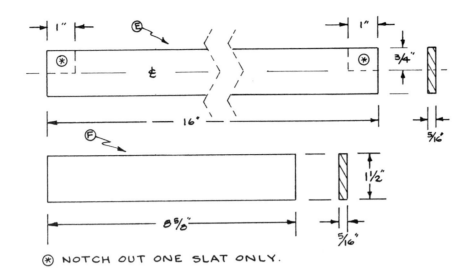

⊛ NOTCH OUT ONE SLAT ONLY.

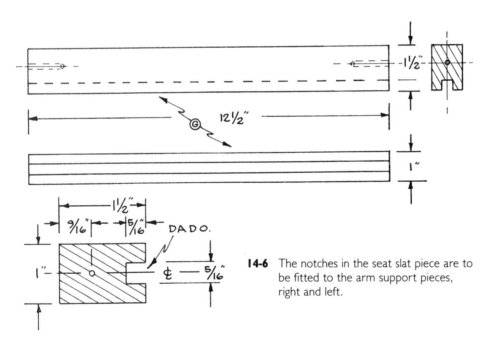

14-6 The notches in the seat slat piece are to be fitted to the arm support pieces, right and left.

Space these slats as shown in FIG. 14-3. Use waterproof glue and secure them in place with #18 × 3/4-inch wire brads. The back subassembly is now completed.

FINAL ASSEMBLY

Align one of the side subassemblies with one end of a back subassembly. Pass the two wood screws through the countersunk holes and into their pilot holes previously drilled into the ends of pieces (G). Tighten these screws securely, top and bottom. Attach the opposite side subassembly to the back subassembly in like manner.

Cut out the notches, as shown in FIG. 14-6, in one seat slat piece (E) only. These notches are to be fitted to the arm support pieces (D), right and left. Place the swing on a solid, flat work surface, and finish-nail the notched slat in place. Next, align a slat piece (E) across the ends of the seat support pieces (C), and finish-nail it securely in place.

Space the remaining four slat pieces (E) about 5/8 of an inch apart, with their ends aligned, and finish-nail them in place.

HANGING THE SWING

Attach two-foot lengths of swing chain to the screw eyes, right and left, with appropriate-size lap links. A *lap link* is a formed chain link which has been cut along one portion at a sharp angle. The resulting ends are spread apart just enough to receive the members to be joined. The link is then closed by placing it against a solid back-up surface and striking it with a hammer.

Attach two more (much longer) lengths of chain to the eye bolts in like manner. Suspend the swing by these longer chains so that it is level. Take the free ends of the shorter front chains, and lift the swing seat so that it is inclined about 5 degrees aft. Hook these front chains to the back chains with two more lap links, and secure them in place.

Adjust for the desired distance between swing seat and the ground by taking up or letting out a few links of the main suspension chains. This adjustment, too, can be secured by the use of lap links. These links can be opened for later adjustments, if necessary, by engaging the cutting edges of a pair of diagonal cutting pliers with the mating surfaces of the diagonally cut lap in the link and forcing them apart.

If rope is chosen for suspension, substitute the proper size thimbles instead of the lap links described above. Free ends of the rope should be bound with a serving of strong twine or string, to which a coating of shellac is applied.

15
Ball
gum dispenser

This neat little ball gum dispenser is ideal as a gift item, both to give and to sell. It is well received by the youngsters, especially, since it works every time—and without a coin (FIG. 15-1).

Material costs for this project are at an absolute minimum. One can hardly call any surplus materials "scrap," when such an item as this little jewel contains only 10 cubic inches of wood! It is an ideal item to offer in kit form, too, together with a copy of "how-to-do-it" notes and illustrations.

INSTRUCTIONS

Study the accompanying drawings, FIGS. 15-2 through 15-6, along with the Materials List, before starting this project. Notice that part A and the base piece (F), can be radiused and grooved with the same setup. Two of the guide parts (C) are required per unit. All the parts are cut from standard 3/4-inch-thick material, and all have a 2 3/4-inch dimension in common, except parts E and F.

If you make two or more articles, make up drill templates or drill jigs for the several drilling operations required. The vertical pilot holes common to parts A, C, D, and into part F must be in alignment for final assembly.

CONTAINER BASE

Cut the top piece (A) to 2 3/4 inches × 2 3/4 inches, but leave it a bit on the plus side to allow for the sanding of its edges later. Locate the centers for the two pilot holes and for the 7/8-inch-diameter hole through its center. It might be necessary to secure this part onto the face plate of your lathe in order to accomplish the 30-degree cut. Notice that it is 1 3/4 inches in diameter at the top surface and 7/8 of an inch in diameter at the bottom.

Wait to accomplish the 3/16-inch radius at the top, as well as the 1/16-inch × 1/16-inch kerf, until after the base (F) has been cut out. Complete both the container base and the base (A and F) with the same setups.

Cut the irregular lobe in the container base (A) as shown. Its width extends to 1/2 an inch from the centerline and parallel to it. Its length extends to 3/8 of an inch on either side of center, allowing a total travel of stop screw S of 3/4 of an inch.

Ball Gum Dispenser

Materials List

No. Req.	Part	Name	Thick	Wide	Long	Remarks
1	A	Container base	3/4″	2³/4″	2³/4″	
1	B	Dispenser	3/4″	1¹/4″	2³/4″	
2	C	Guides	3/4″	3/4″	2³/4″	
1	D	Ejector	3/4″	2³/4″	2³/4″	
1	F	Base	3/4″	3¹/2″	3¹/2″	
1	E	Incline	See Fig. 15-4			

Supplies/Hardware

1	Small glass jar, with threaded top (Fig. 15-6)
1	Felt for base piece E, ¹/16″ × 3¹/2″ × 3 1/2″
1	Wood bead, drilled, 3/4″. Pull knob (Fig. 15-6)
1	Oval-head Phillips wood screw, #6 × 1″ Pull knob
2	Round-head wood screws, #6 × 2³/4″
3″	#12 or #14 copper wire
2	Binder-head, self-tapping screws
1	#6 round-head wood screw × 3/4″, S stop screw

15-1   Ball gum dispenser.

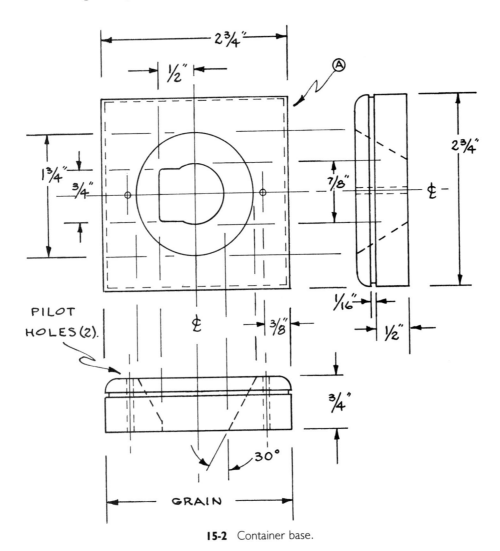

15-2 Container base.

DISPENSER SLIDING PIECE

Cut out the dispenser piece (B) as shown in FIG. 15-3. Locate the 3/4-inch-diameter hole in its center and drill or hole-saw it through. Bevel-cut or sand its top diameter at 45 degrees to 7/8 inch in diameter. Locate and drill the pilot hole for the #6 Phillips screw which is to retain the pull knob.

Two guide pieces (C) are required per assembly, as shown in FIGS. 15-3 and 15-6. Cut out and drill these for later assembly.

EJECTOR PIECE

The ejector piece (D) embodies the ejection chute for the gum balls. Cut it to size as shown in FIG. 15-4, and locate the center for the 3/4-inch diameter hole. Drill this hole through. Cut out a 3/4-inch × 3/4-inch opening to intercept this hole.

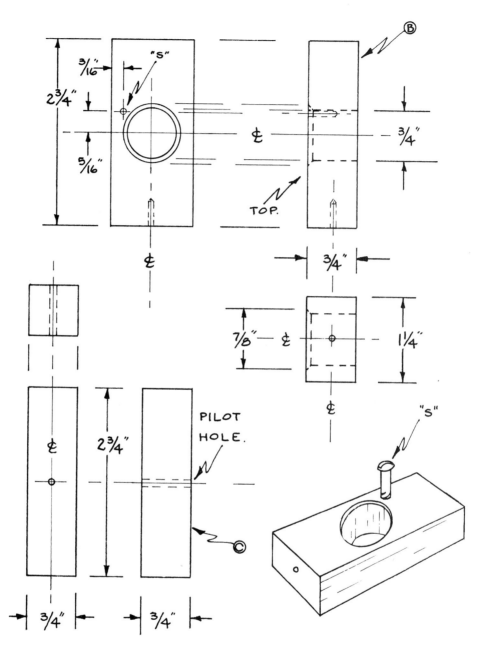

15-3 Locate the 3/4-inch-diameter hole in the center of the dispenser piece (B) and drill it through.

Sand an incline into the top surface of the part (D) and on the inside circumference of the hole, at about 30 degrees for a distance of 1/8 of an inch, as indicated. Wrap a piece of sandpaper around a short length of dowel rod to accomplish this cut.

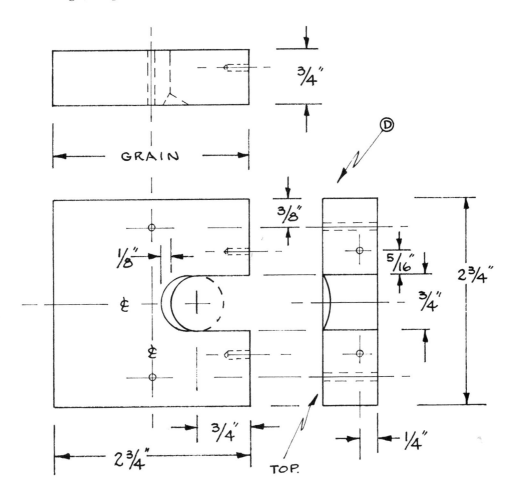

GRAIN

3/4"

3/8"

1/8"

5/16"

2 3/4"

3/4"

3/4"

1/4"

2 3/4"

TOP.

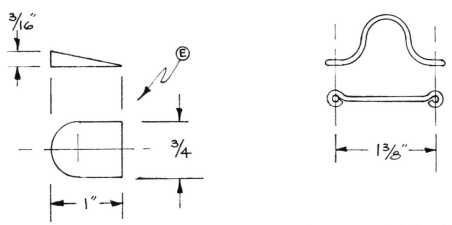

3/16"

3/4

1"

1 3/8"

15-4 Cut the ejector piece to size, locate and drill a 3/4-inch-diameter hole through it.

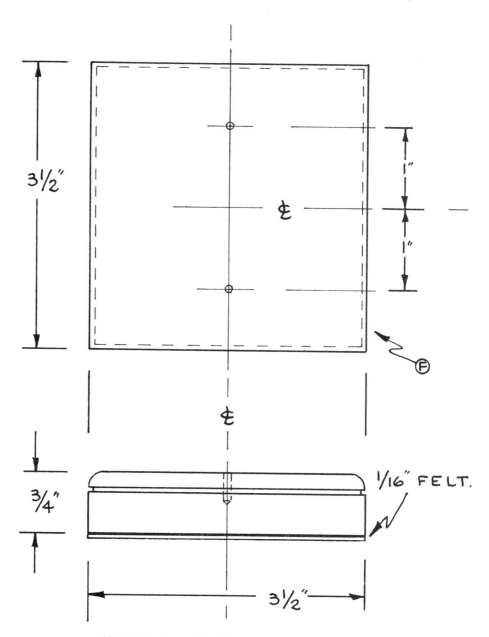

15-5 Note the relationship of the dispenser to the base.

Locate and drill the two continuing alignment holes, then locate and drill the pilot holes for the binder head screws which will retain the wire catcher loop later.

Piece E is a small inclined plane which assures that the released gum ball will travel out of the chute and into the wire catcher loop.

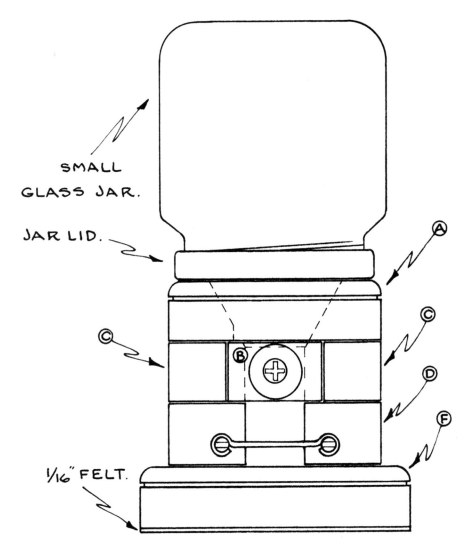

SMALL
GLASS JAR.

JAR LID.

Ⓐ

Ⓒ

Ⓑ

Ⓒ

Ⓓ

Ⓕ

1/16" FELT.

15-6 Stack the container/base (A), the dispenser (B), the two guides (C), and the ejector piece (D).

BASE PIECE

Cut out the base piece (F) to $3^{1}/_{2} \times 3^{1}/_{2}$ inches as shown in FIG. 15-5. Locate and drill the two pilot holes. Note that the holes in this piece (F) are only about $1/_{4}$-inch in depth.

Set up to rout or shape the $3/_{16}$-inch radii and the $1/_{16}$-inch $\times$ $1/_{16}$-inch kerfs at this time. Accomplish these operations on components F and A with the same setup.

SUBASSEMBLY

Stack the container/base (A), the dispenser (B), the two guides (C), and the ejector piece (D) as shown in FIG. 15-6. Clamp them together and line-drill through the previously drilled pilot holes so as to accommodate the #6 × 2³/4-inch round head wood screws.

This done, disassemble these pieces while keeping them in order. Sand the surfaces of the sliding piece (B) slightly to provide a slip-fit within its opening. Reassemble pieces A, C, and D, applying a small amount of glue to their mating surfaces. Temporarily install the two screws through the pieces to assure their alignment, and clamp them in place until the glue has set.

Sand the outside surfaces of this subassembly smooth and to conformity. This is much easier to accomplish now than after final assembly. Slip the dispenser piece (B) into place and retain it with a #6 × ³/4-inch round head wood screw S to a depth of about half its threaded portion (FIG. 15-3). Push piece B into the sub-assembly until its travel is stopped by the screw S. Check again that its end surfaces are flush with the fore and aft surfaces of the subassembly. If not, adjust and/or sand as necessary.

FINAL ASSEMBLY

Choose a small glass jar with a threaded lid, approximately as shown in FIG. 15-6. Cut a 1³/4-inch-diameter hole in the center of the lid. Locate and drill two holes 180 degrees apart and on a one-inch radius about the center. These holes are for the #6 round head screws. Paint the lid now, if desired.

Invert the lid on top of the previously completed subassembly, and align the screw holes. Insert the two #6 screws through the lid, the subassembly, and into the two pilot-drilled holes in the base piece (F). Tighten these screws securely. Place a drop of glue on the incline piece (E) and push into the chute in the ejector piece (D) and against the base piece (F).

Countersink one end of the hole through a wood bead, and install it on the front of the sliding piece (B) with an oval head #6 Phillips screw. This serves as the pull knob.

Form a short length of copper wire as shown in FIG. 15-4. Install it as a "catcher" for the gum balls, using two #6 binder head self-tapping screws.

The prototype dispenser was shot with clear acrylic spray at this point, to reveal the natural wood grain and colors. Obviously, any color coating desired may be applied.

Apply glue to the bottom of the base piece (F) and install a 3¹/2-inch × 3¹/2-inch piece of ¹/16-inch-thick felt to the bottom.

Fill the glass jar with gum balls and screw it in place into its modified lid. Your miniature gum ball dispenser is now ready for service.

16
Rocky duck

Rocky duck is a sturdy, inexpensive, and easy-to-make riding toy that will delight the preschool set. Excellent rocking surfaces are provided by the curvature of the wings. The 2 × 12 material used makes for a wider "tread" and thus for easier operation on carpeted floors. This design also eliminates any need for cross-bracing between the rockers. The "tail feathers" near the wing tips serve to prevent overly eager little rockers from tipping over backward (FIG. 16-1).

INSTRUCTIONS

Start this project by laying out a full scale pattern for the wings (A) as shown in FIGS. 16-2 and 16-3. Align these figures along their match line to obtain a complete pattern. Lay out a one-inch grid on a piece of heavy paper at least 11¹/₂ inches × 27 inches, and transfer the outline of the wing onto this grid.

THE WINGS

Cut out one wing piece (A) from standard 2 × 12 material (1¹/₂ inches × 11¹/₄ inches). Use this wing to trace around and cut out a second wing piece. Two wings can be cut out from a four-foot piece of material by overlapping the wing tips. Stack these two wings and sand them to conformity on a belt sander.

At this point, there is no difference between a right and a left wing, so choose the better surfaces for outside exposure. Locate and drill the one-inch-diameter holes for the support rod (C) to a depth of 1¹/₈ inches only, and on the inside surfaces of the wings. Locate and drill through the two holes in each wing for the #12 × 3¹/₂ inch flat head wood screws. Countersink these holes on the outside surface of each wing piece.

Cut out the tail feather pieces (D) and trace the curve of the wing onto them for a net fit. Glue and finish-nail these onto the wings, right and left, as shown in FIG. 16-4.

THE HEAD

Lay out a pattern for the head piece (B), following FIG. 16-5, and in the same manner as the wing outline. Cut out a head piece from 2 × 12 material and locate the

Rocky Duck

Materials List

No. Req.	Part	Name	Thick	Wide	Long	Remarks
2	A	Wings	$1^1/2''$	$11^1/4''$	27"	Standard 2 × 12
1	B	Head	$1^1/2''$	10"	$11^1/4''$	
1	C	Support rod	1" dia.		$13^1/2''$	Dowel rod
2	D	Tail feathers	$3/4''$	$1^1/2''$	$7^5/8''$	
1	E	Handle	$3/4''$ dia.		$6^3/4''$	Dowel rod
1	F	Seat	$1^1/2''$	$11^1/4''$	17"	Standard 2 × 12
1	G	Seat back	$1/2''$	$11^1/4''$	$10^5/8''$	Plywood
1	H	Foot rest	$1/2''$	$11^1/4''$	$6^1/2''$	
1	J	Leg rest	$1/2''$	$11^1/4''$	$7^3/4''$	
1	K	Bumper	$1^1/2''$	$2^1/4''$	$7^3/8''$	

Hardware

2	#12 × 4" flat-head wood screws
4	#12 × $3^1/2''$ flat-head wood screws
2	#10 × $2^1/2''$ flat-head wood screws

16-1 Rocky duck.

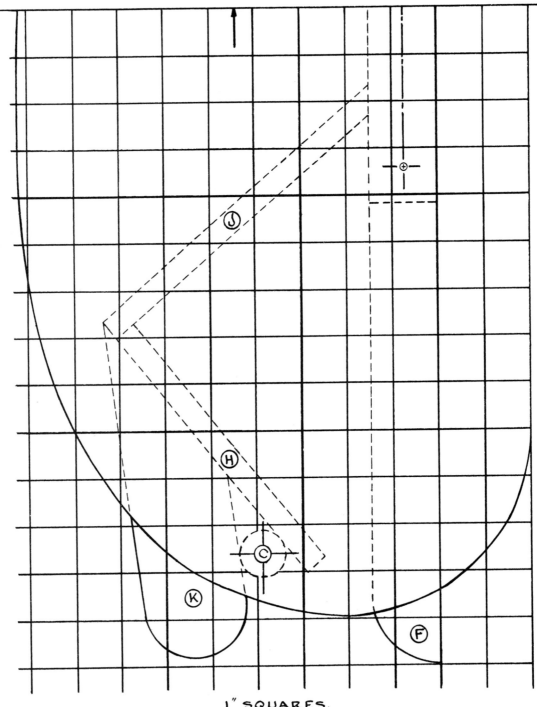

I" SQUARES.

PART Ⓐ.

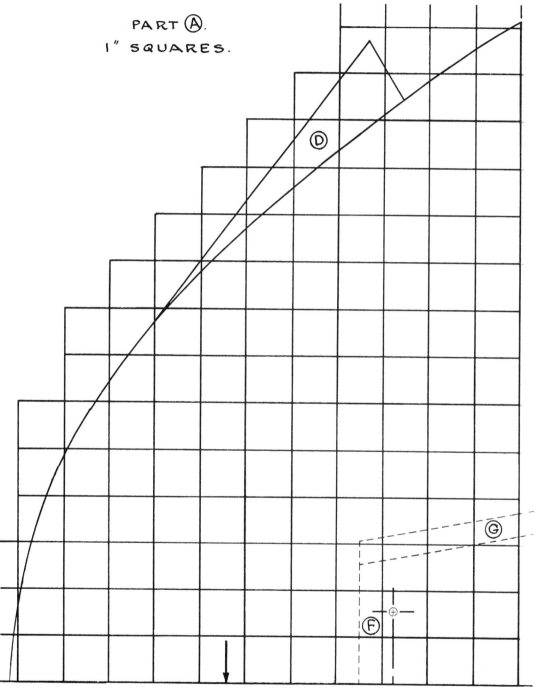

16-2 and 16-3 Start this project by laying out a full-scale pattern for the wings (A).

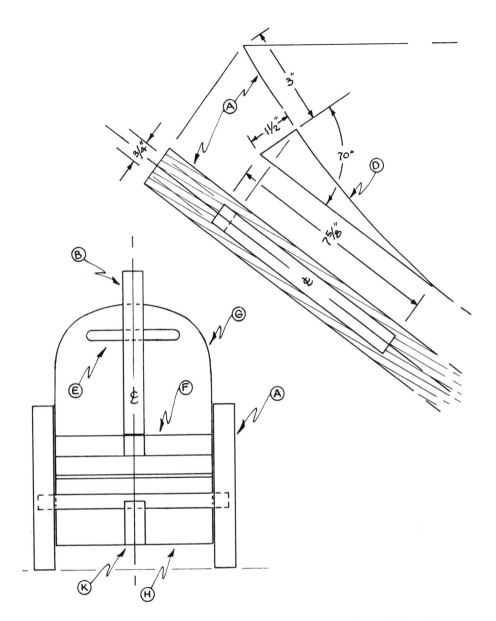

16-4 Glue and finish-nail the tail feather pieces onto the wings, right and left, as shown.

3/4-inch hole for the handle (E) and the one-inch hole for the eye. Pilot-drill through these locations with a 1/8-inch-diameter drill bit. Follow these pilot holes with the appropriate bits to a depth of about one inch only. Turn the workpiece over and follow the pilot hole through. This procedure leaves a clean hole on both sides of the workpiece.

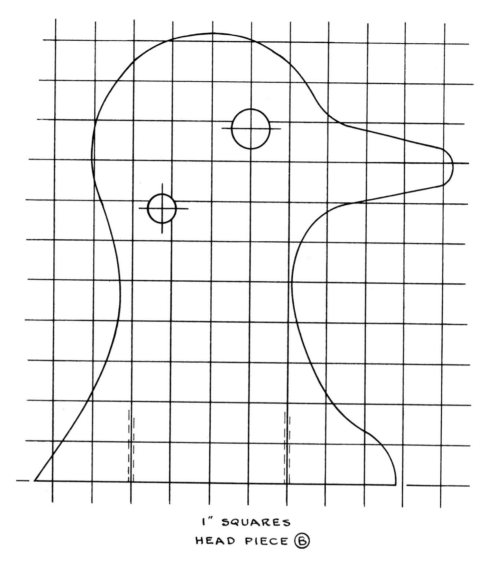

I" SQUARES
HEAD PIECE Ⓑ

16-5 Lay out a pattern for the head piece (B) as you did for the wing outline.

Lay out and drill pilot holes for the #12 × four-inch flat head wood screws on the underneath surface of the head piece, on the centerline, as shown in FIGS. 16-5 and 16-6.

THE SEAT

Lay out and cut the seat piece (F) as shown in FIGS. 16-6 and 16-7. Radius the lower front end of this piece at 1¹/2 inches to conform to the curve of the head piece. Bevel the back edge of the seat at 10 degrees.

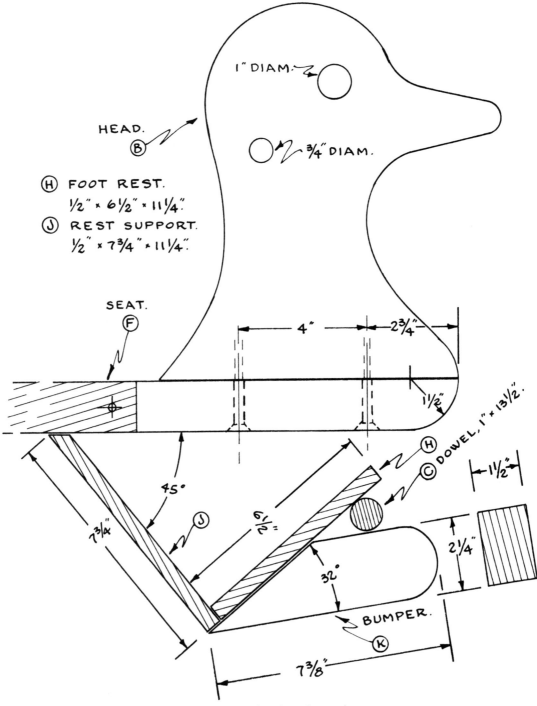

16-6 Note how the pieces fit together.

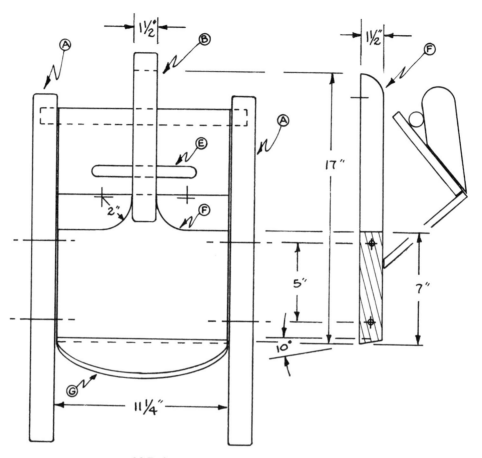

16-7 Lay out and cut the seat piece (F).

Locate and drill the two holes for attaching the head piece. Countersink these holes on the underneath surface. Locate and drill the two pilot holes on each side of the seat piece for the wing attaching screws.

Lay out and cut the seat back piece (G) as shown in FIG. 16-8, from 1/2-inch plywood.

THE SEAT SUBASSEMBLY

Align the seat back piece with the aft edge of the seat (F). Apply glue to the mating surfaces and nail or screw the back (G) to the seat. Align the head piece (B) with the seat and apply glue to their mating surfaces. Draw these two pieces tightly together with the #12 × four-inch wood screws.

Cut a 6³/4-inch length of ³/4-inch-diameter dowel rod for the handle (E). Turn a spherical radius on each end of the handle piece. Push it into the ³/4-inch hole previously drilled through the head piece (B). Apply wood glue to the handle at

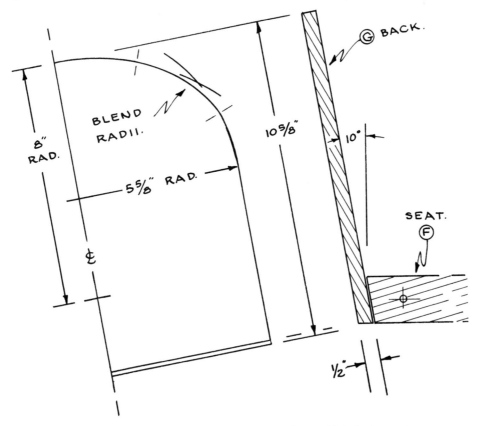

16-8 Lay out and cut the seat back piece (G) from 1/2-inch plywood.

about its center area, and gently rotate it into position so as to leave 2⅝ inches on either side of the head.

THE FOOTREST SUBASSEMBLY

Cut out the footrest (H) and the legrest (J) from 1/2-inch plywood as shown in FIGS. 16-6 and 16-7. Cut out a bumper piece (K). Apply wood glue to the mating surfaces between the bumper piece and the footrest, and nail or screw these pieces together securely.

Align the legrest (J) with the aft edge of the footrest piece (H). Glue and finish-nail these components together. Lay these subassemblies aside for a time until the glue has set up properly.

FINAL ASSEMBLY

Cut a 13½-inch length of one-inch-diameter dowel rod and chamfer both ends of it to form the support rod (C). Apply glue to one end of this rod, and press it into the hole provided for it in the left wing piece (A).

Align the seat subassembly just completed with the left wing attaching holes. Apply glue to the mating surfaces, and install the retaining screws securely in place.

Next, fit the footrest and bumper subassembly into place. Hold these components firmly against the bottom of the seat piece (F) and drill two holes through the aft edge of the legrest (J) and into the seat. Countersink these holes in the legrest (J) and into the seat. Countersink these holes in the legrest (J) for two #10 × 2¹/₂-inch flat-head wood screws. Glue and screw these components together.

Finally, apply wood glue to the remaining end of the support rod piece (C) and to the remaining mating surfaces. Align the right wing with the rod (C) and with the attaching holes in the seat (F). Install the retaining wood screws securely in place. Drive two small finishing nails through the footrest and into the support rod.

Sand all exposed surfaces and corners smoothly, and finish the completed assembly as desired. Rocky Duck is now ready for years of faithful service.

17

Small wheelbarrow

This sturdy and attractive wheelbarrow design is easy to construct, requires minimal materials, and can also be very useful. It can serve as a vehicle for floral displays or for your prized potted specimens. At the same time, it makes it easier for one to move a plant from one location to another.

You will also want to make one of these as a toy to delight the kindergarten set—it is just their size. The chances are that you already have enough material around the shop to make two of them, anyway (FIG. 17-1).

INSTRUCTIONS

Although this is a comparatively simple project design, it would be well to read through this chapter before beginning the project, referring to the several figures and notes as well. As always, refer to the Materials List to identify the parts by their assigned letters. While almost any choice of woods will do nicely, one might want to consider oak (or other hardwoods), and a stain-and-varnish finish.

If the completed item is to be used for potted plants, you should try to use waterproof glue and exterior-grade plywood.

THE HANDLE SUBASSEMBLY

First, cut the handles (A) to $1^1/4$ inches × $1^1/4$ inches × 30 inches long, as shown in FIGS. 17-2 and 17-3. Locate the centers on each end of these two pieces and turn one end of each, as shown. Locate and drill a $3/4$-inch-diameter hole, $3/4$ inch deep, on the centerline of each handle piece and at $10^1/4$ inches from their turned ends.

Cut two pieces of one-inch-diameter dowel rod stock, $4^3/4$ inches long, for the legs (B). Turn a $3/4$-inch tenon on one end of each leg, $3/4$ inch long. Turn a radius on the opposite (lower) ends as desired. Chamfer the tenons, apply wood glue to them, and press them into the holes previously drilled in the handles (A). Up until this point, these subassemblies are either right-hand or left-hand.

Drill a $1/8$-inch-diameter pilot hole through each handle piece, two inches from their square (front) ends, as shown in FIG. 17-3. These holes are to be drilled

Small Wheelbarrow

Materials List

No. Req.	Part	Name	Thick	Wide	Long	Remarks
2	A	Handles	1¹/₄"	1¹/₄"	30"	
2	B	Legs	1" dia.		4³/₄"	Dowel rod
1	C	Bottom	³/₄"	11¹/₄"	14"	1 × 12, or ³/₄" plywood
1	D	Front end	³/₄"	4³/₄"	5"	
2	E	Sides	³/₄"	5¹/₂"	14⁷/₈"	
1	F	Wheel	1¹/₂"	8" dia.		
1	G	Axle	1" dia.		3¹/₂"	Dowel rod

Hardware

4	#10 × 1¹/₂" flat-head wood screws, brass
2	³/₁₆" × 2¹/₂" round-head wood screws, brass

at 7¹/₂ degrees, on the centerlines. Be certain to keep the proper relationship between these holes and the legs, as this relative positioning is what determines which is right-hand and which is left-hand.

Using a ³/₈-inch paddle blade bit, follow these pilot holes from the outside surfaces of the legs to a depth of ¹/₄ of an inch only. Then drill through with a ³/₁₆-inch bit.

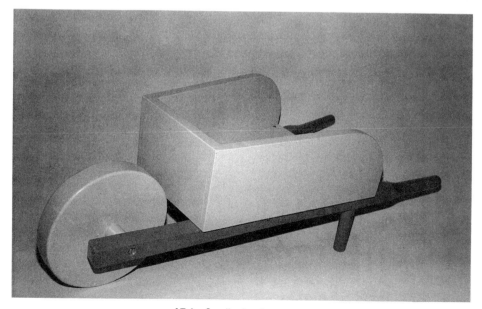

17-1 Small wheelbarrow.

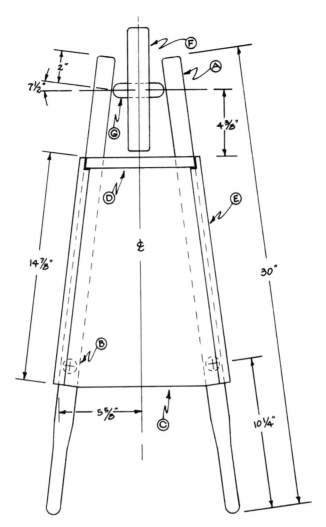

17-2 Cut the handles (A) to 1¹/4 inches square × 30 inches long.

THE WHEEL AND AXLE

Cut out the eight-inch-diameter wheel from 1¹/2-inch stock. Radius the circumference as desired. Drill a pilot hole through the center of the wheel and follow it with a one-inch paddle blade bit to a depth of about one inch. Turn the wheel over and follow the pilot hole again, until the one-inch diameters intercept.

Cut a 3¹/2-inch length of one-inch-diameter dowel rod for the axle (G) and turn a spherical radius on each end. Locate the centers and drill pilot holes for the ³/16-inch axle screws to be installed later. Center and glue the axle (G) in the wheel (F), as shown in FIGS. 17-2 and 17-4.

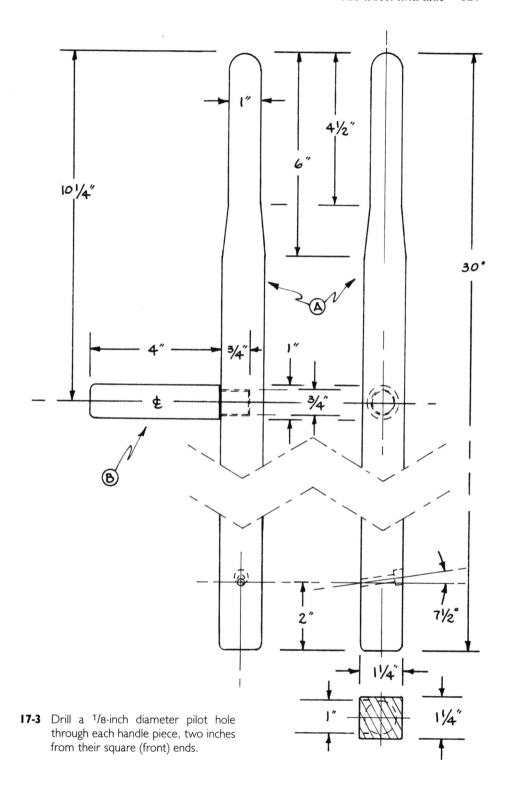

17-3 Drill a ¹/₈-inch diameter pilot hole through each handle piece, two inches from their square (front) ends.

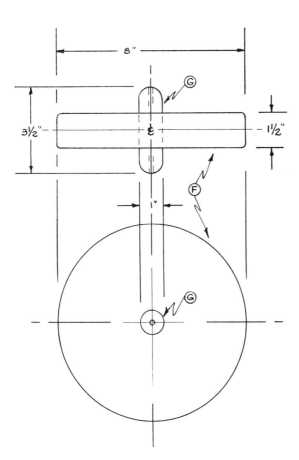

17-4 Center and glue the axle (G)
in the wheel (F).

THE BOX COMPONENTS

Cut out two side pieces (E) from 3/4-inch material as shown in FIG. 17-5. Stack them and cut the four-inch radius on one corner of each piece.

Cut out the bottom piece (C) as shown in FIG. 17-6, from standard 1 × 12 material, or from exterior grade 3/4-inch plywood. The two outside edges of this piece are to be cut at an angle 7$\frac{1}{2}$ degrees, with respect to the centerline. Locate, drill through, and countersink the four holes for the #10 wood screws.

Cut a 3/8 × 3/8-inch rabbet along the side edges of the bottom piece. With this same setup, cut the rabbet along the longer (lower) edges of the two side pieces (E). Be sure to run these two pieces through the saw from opposite ends, or you will wind up with two left-hand (or two right-hand) pieces.

Rip the front end piece (D) to width, then tilt the saw blade to 82$\frac{1}{2}$ degrees to trim the ends to length. While the saw blade is thus tilted, make the 3/8-inch deep cuts in the two side pieces, 3/4 of an inch from their front ends. To complete these angled rabbets, either edge-cut the pieces or waste out the material with dado blades. Clean the cuts up with a sharp chisel as may be necessary.

These angled rabbets must be on the same (inside) surfaces of the side pieces as the 3/8-inch × 3/8-inch rabbets previously cut in their lower edges.

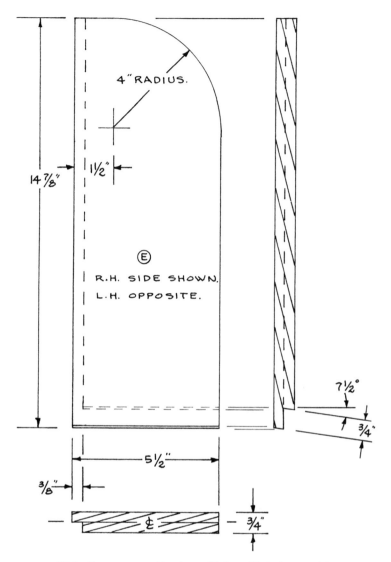

17-5 Cut out two side pieces (E) from 3/4-inch material.

THE HANDLE SUBASSEMBLY

Pass an axle-retaining screw through the 3/16-inch hole in the handle (A), from the counter-bored (outside) end of the hole. Align this screw with the pilot hole in one end of the axle and tighten it, while allowing for free rotation of the wheel and axle. Pass the remaining axle screw through the opposite handle in like manner, and tighten it in the other end of the axle as before.

If this subassembly is to be finished differently from the box, it may be sanded and color-coated (or stained and clear-coated) at this time.

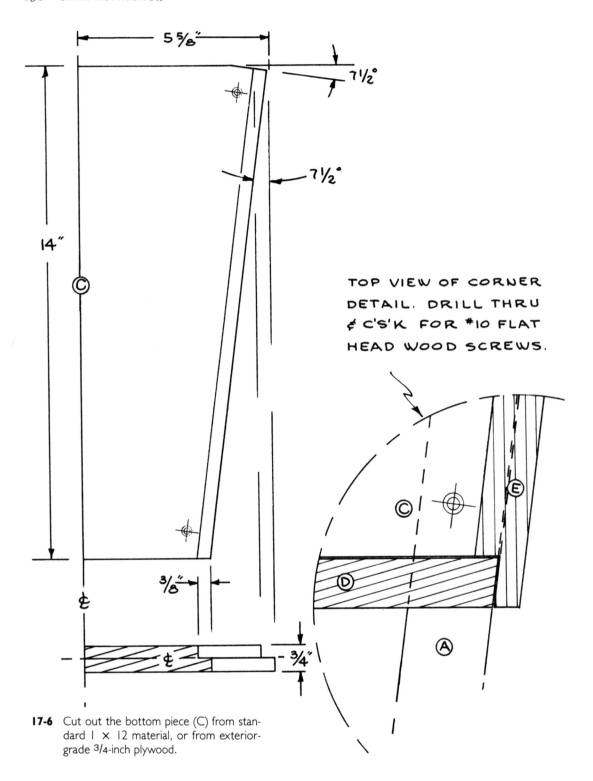

5 5/8"

7 1/2°

7 1/2°

14"

©C

3/8"

3/4"

TOP VIEW OF CORNER
DETAIL. DRILL THRU
& C'S'K FOR #10 FLAT
HEAD WOOD SCREWS.

©E

©C

©D

©A

17-6 Cut out the bottom piece (C) from standard 1 × 12 material, or from exterior-
grade 3/4-inch plywood.

THE BOX SUBASSEMBLY

Align the front end piece (D) with the front edge of the bottom piece (C) as shown in FIG. 17-2. Waterproof glue and finish-nail these pieces together.

Align the two side pieces (E), right and left, with the edges of the bottom piece (C) and with the ends of the front piece (D). Waterproof glue and finish-nail these components securely together to complete the box unit. This subassembly may now be sanded and finished as desired.

FINAL ASSEMBLY

Place the completed box unit on the handle subassembly. The wheelbarrow should now stand alone on a flat work surface. Align the wheel (F) with the centerline of the front piece (D), leaving $3/8$ of an inch clearance between the wheel and the front end of the box unit.

The handles should be parallel with the sides (E). The bottom edges of the two sides will overhang the handles by about $3/8$ of an inch, right and left. Reach through the screw holes in the bottom piece with an awl, and mark the locations for the pilot holes to be drilled in the handles. Pilot-drill these four holes, and install the box onto the handles with the four #10 flat head wood screws. This completes the final assembly of the wheelbarrow.

The prototype wheelbarrow was finished in a two-tone color scheme. The handles/legs/wheel portion was gloss enameled in avocado green, while the box unit was finished in an almond enamel.

Any solid color (or combination of colors) may be applied as desired. If hardwood, such as oak, is used in construction, you might want to stain and spar-varnish the entire project.

18

Children's desk or magazine rack

These attractive and versatile children's desks can also serve as flower pot displays, for books, for a lamp, as end tables—even as magazine racks with modification, as you will see. The desks are quite sturdy without the need for cross-bracing, and no special hardware is required in their construction. They are made from standard 1 × 12 lumber, for the most part (FIGS. 18-1, 18-2, and 18-3).

You'll want to make a template or pattern piece for the compound side units (D—E) from 1/8-inch wall paneling or Masonite sheet. Both of these parts can be cut from the same 20-inch length of 1 × 12 (FIG. 18-4), as can a few of the required support pieces, as well.

INSTRUCTIONS

Cut out two of each of the side components (D and E) as shown in FIG. 18-4. Edge-glue one of each of these pieces together along their common line to form complete side units, two of which are required per assembly. The units so formed are neither right-hand nor left-hand, thus far, so choose their better surfaces for outside exposure at this time. This is especially important if the completed project is to be stained and clear-coated.

THE SIDE SUBASSEMBLIES

Cut out two pieces each of the desk-top support (G) and the seat support piece (F), as shown in FIG. 18-5. One end of each of these pieces is bevel cut at 10 degrees, while their opposite ends are radiused. Notice that pieces F and G differ, however, in the relationship between the bevel cuts and the radii—as well as in their overall lengths.

Locate one of each of these support pieces on the inside surface of a completed side unit (D and E). Glue and finish-nail them in place. Follow the same procedure on the opposite side unit, being careful to end up with a matching right-hand and a left-hand pair of sides.

Cut two pieces of the base strip (H) as shown in FIG. 18-5 to the desired length. Their length will depend on the end use to be made of the completed desk. For

Child's Desk or Magazine Rack

Materials List

No. Req.	Part	Name	Thick	Wide	Long	Remarks
1	A	Desk top	$3/4$"	$11^1/4$"	16"	Fig. 32-6
1	B*	Seat back	$3/4$"	8"	16"	
1	C*	Seat	$3/4$"	9"	16"	
2	D	Side unit	$3/4$"	10"	20"	Fig. 32-3
2	E*	Side unit	$3/4$"	$4^5/8$"	10"	
2	F	Seat support	$3/4$"	1"	11"	Fig. 32-5
2	G	Top support	$3/4$"	1"	$10^3/4$"	
2	H	Base pieces	$3/4$"	$1^1/2$"	As desired	

Magazine Rack Configuration*

No. Req.	Part	Name	Thick	Wide	Long	Remarks
2	D*	Modified side unit	$3/4$"	10"	20"	Fig. 32-4
1	J*	Rack bottom	$1/4$"	$4^{11}/16$"	$13^3/4$"	Fig. 32-6
3	K*	Rack slats	$1/4$"	$1^1/2$"	16"	Fig. 32-5
2	L*	Seat/rack support	$3/4$"	1"	13"	
2	H*	Base pieces	$3/4$"	$1^1/2$"	As desired	Figs. 32-1, -2, and -5

18-1A Child's desk.

18-2B Child's desk with magazine rack.

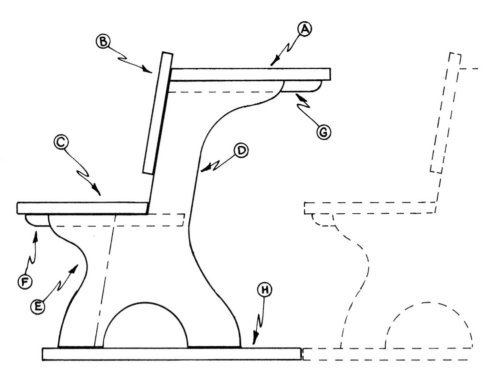

18-2 The single desk uses base pieces 18 inches long, with one inch extending ahead of the front "leg."

instance, the single desk (FIG. 18-2) uses base pieces 18 inches long, with one inch extending ahead of the front "leg." Two desks, or a desk and a magazine rack configuration, may be placed in tandem. They can be joined together via longer base pieces or left as independent units.

Assuming that you follow the configuration in FIG. 18-2, align the legs of the side units on the centerlines of the base pieces (H), right and left. Glue and finish-nail or screw them in place. You will now have completed a pair of side subassemblies.

DESK TOP, SEAT, AND BACK

Cut a desk top piece (A) from standard 1 × 12 material, 3/4-inch × 11 1/4 inches × 16 inches. Bevel one 16-inch edge at 10 degrees as shown in FIG. 18-6. The seat piece is the same, except that it is only nine inches wide. The seat back piece (B) is 3/4-inch × 8 inches × 16 inches.

Scribe a light pencil line on the underneath sides of all three of these pieces, 3/8-inch from each end and parallel to it. These guidelines are for final assembly of the desk.

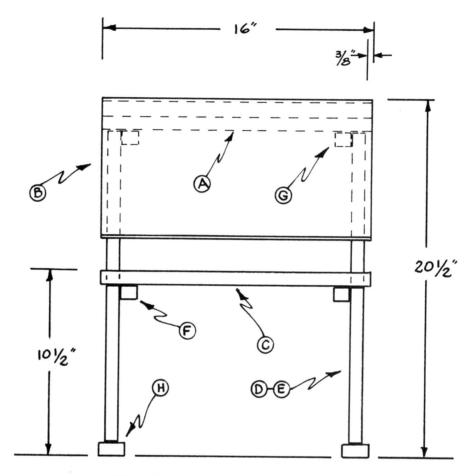

18-3 Guidelines are for final assembly of the desk.

FINAL ASSEMBLY

Place a seat piece (C) upside down on the edge of a flat, clean work surface. Align a side subassembly with the appropriate 3/8-inch guidelines described above. Index the back edge (10-degree bevel) of the seat with the 10-degree inclination of the side unit (D). Glue and finish-nail or screw the seat in place. Follow the same procedure with the remaining (opposite) side subassembly.

Next, place a desk top piece (A) upside down on the work surface. Index the front (10-degree bevel) edge of the top with the 10-degree inclination of the side units (D), and with the guidelines scribed 3/8-inch from each end of the desk top. Glue and finish-nail or screw these pieces together. The unit thus formed will now rest steadily on its base pieces (H).

Finally, fit a back piece (B) in place so that its top edge is one inch above, and parallel to, the desk top (A). Pilot-drill two finishing nail holes through the seat

18-4 Both of these parts can be cut from the same 20-inch length of 1 × 12 along with a few of the required support pieces, as well.

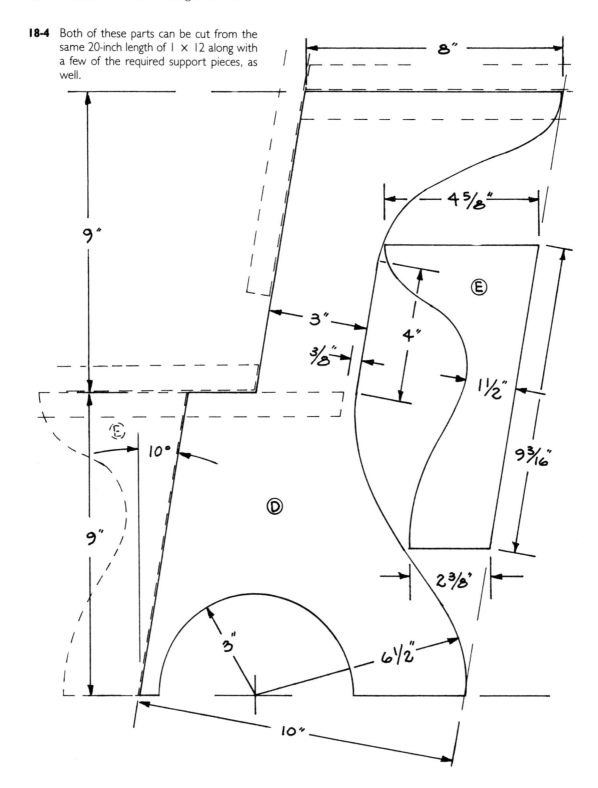

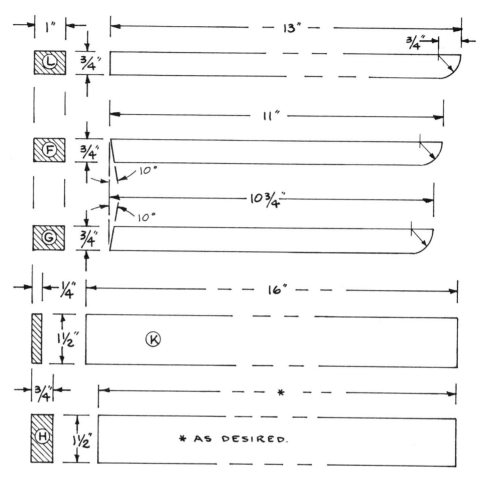

18-5 Cut out two pieces each of the desk top support (G) and the seat support piece (F).

back (B) and into the front edge of top (A), near the upper corners, right and left. The best "drill" for a net fit for any nail is a nail. Cut the head off the nail and chuck it into your drill. This procedure also precludes any splitting of the wood when final nailing is accomplished.

Temporarily install a nail through each of these holes so that it just penetrates the desk top for now.

Align the back with the side units, following the previously scribed guidelines. Again, drill pilot holes through the seat back (B) and into the side unit parts (D), right and left, near the bottom of the back piece. Remove the fitted back and apply wood glue to the mating surfaces. Nail the back in place and set the nails. Notice that this final procedure lends great rigidity to the completed desk assembly.

THE MAGAZINE RACK

While two or more of the desks may be placed in tandem for the children, sooner or later one is going to see the need for a "caboose" on the train. This is where

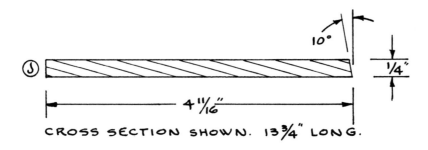

CROSS SECTION SHOWN. 13¾" LONG.

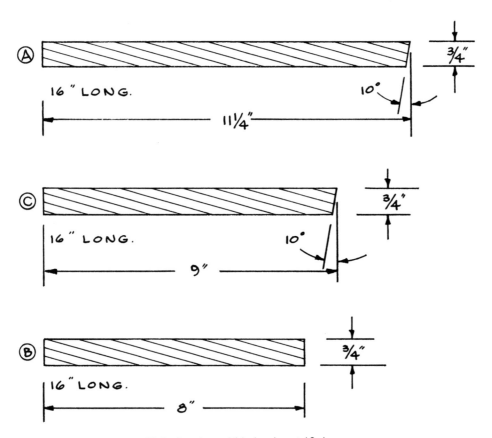

18-6   Bevel one 16-inch edge at 10 degrees.

the magazine rack configuration enters the picture.

The side units (D*) are similar to desk side units, except as shown in FIG. 18-7. Side components (E) are the same for either of the configurations. Parts A and G are not used, and new parts (J, K, and L) are added. Follow essentially the same procedures as in building a desk unit, with the following four exceptions:

18-7 The side units (D*) are similar to the desk side units, except as shown here.

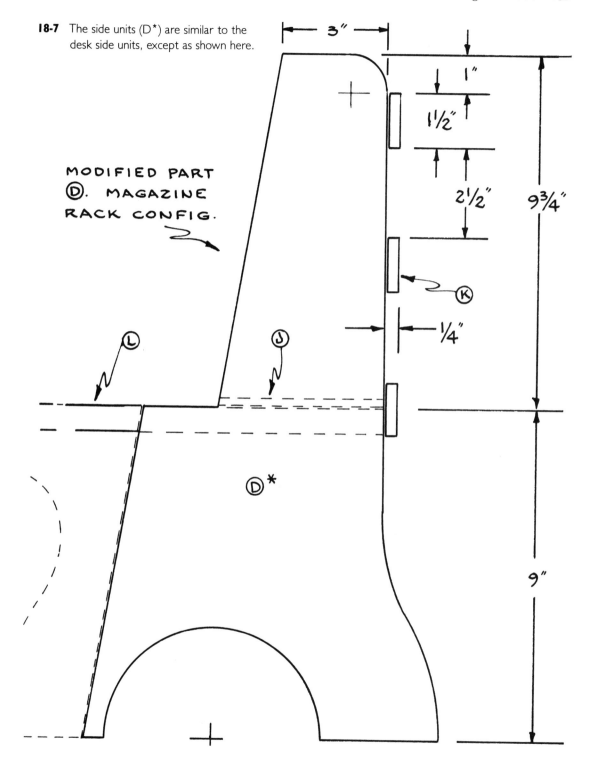

MODIFIED PART Ⓓ. MAGAZINE RACK CONFIG.

3"

1"

1½"

2½"

9¾"

¼"

Ⓚ

Ⓛ

Ⓙ

Ⓓ*

9"

1. After edge-gluing parts D* and E together, install the two seat rack supports, right and left, so that their square ends are flush with the aft edges of parts D*.

2. Join these subassemblies by installing the seat (C) as previously described. Index the seat back (B) so that its top edge is one inch above the tops of parts D* on either side. Glue and nail it in place.

3. Install the rack bottom piece (J) so that its 10-degree bevel edge is against the aft edge of the seat (C). Glue and wire-brad it into place on the rack bottom, right and left.

4. Align and install the three rack slats (K) as shown in FIG. 18-7, using wood glue and small finishing nails.

These versatile and useful articles will make attractive additions to almost any decor. Children will enjoy their own units for play, for drawing and reading, for book storage, snacking, watching TV, etc., for many years to come.

19

Rocking horse

This rocking horse project will provide years of delightful service and enjoyment to the diaper and toddler set. I made mine from birch plywood and oak, and it has proven to be rugged enough to meet the demands of the most energetic of little cowpokes (FIG. 19-1).

The project is composed of more different components than most, as you can see from the Materials List, and the several illustrations. Construction will progress much easier if you go over these carefully before attempting to cut out and assemble the various parts. As always, be sure to note the letters assigned to each piece to ease the construction process.

INSTRUCTIONS

Lay out a one-inch grid pattern on heavy paper, cardboard, or 1/8-inch panel material at least 11 inches × 24 inches. Transfer the outlines from the head and body onto your grid pattern (FIGS. 19-2 and 19-3). Align the two arrow points to make one complete body outline from these two figures.

In like manner, lay out a one-inch grid on a pattern at least 11 inches × 14 inches. Transfer the outlines of the horse's legs, front and rear, onto your pattern, as shown in FIG. 19-4. Two each of these parts (A, B, and C) are required for each rocking horse unit.

Band-saw or jigsaw these components from your chosen material, observing the recommended direction of the surface grains. This will give your steed additional strength and longer service life. Leave the hooves long, as shown. They will be trimmed to the contour of the rockers during final assembly. Locate and pilot-drill the attaching holes.

THE ROCKERS

Place the material for the rockers on the end of a workbench and parallel to it. Use either 5/8-inch or 3/4-inch oak for best results. Extend the centerline from the material to a point 38 inches above the "tread" of each rocker, and scribe an arc. Shorten this radial line to 36 1/2 inches, and again scribe an arc 1 1/2 inches from the first one. Radius the front ends of these rockers at 1 1/2 as shown in FIG. 19-5.

Rocking Horse

Materials List

No. Req.	Part	Name	Thick	Wide	Long	Remarks
2	A	Body	3/4″	12″	23″	7-ply wood
2	B	Rear leg	3/4″	7″	13″	
2	C	Front leg	3/4″	6″	13″	
2	D	Rocker	3/4″	3 1/2″	26″	5/8″ or 3/4″ oak
1	E	Foot rest	5/8″	3 1/4″	12 3/4″	5/8″ oak
1	F	Seat	1/2″	11 1/4″	7 1/4″	1/2″ plywood
1	G	Back	1/2″	11 1/4″	9 5/8″	
2	H	Back support	5/8″	3/4″	5 3/4″	Oak
2	J	Seat support	5/8″	3/4″	6 7/8″	
1	K	Tray	1/2″	5 5/8″	11 1/4″	1/2″ plywood
1	L	Aft support	5/8″	1 1/2″	11 1/4″	Oak
1	M	Front support	1/4″	1 1/4″	11 1/4″	
2	N	Ears	5/8″	7/8″	1 3/4″	

Supplies

4	1/4″ × 1 1/2″ carriage bolts, washers, nuts (legs)
4	1/2″ × 1/2″ 90-degree corner angles (tray)
8	#6 × 1/2″ flat-head wood screws (angles)
2	#6 × 1 1/4″ round-head wood screws (ears)
12	#8 × 1 1/4″ flat-head wood screws (seat, rockers, foot rest)

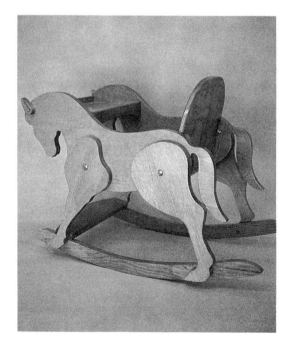

19-1 Rocking horse.

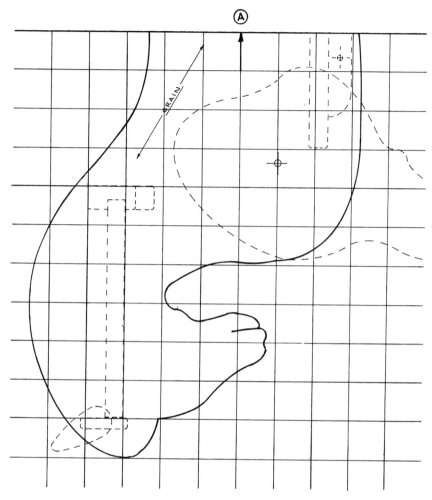

19-2 Transfer the outlines from the head and body onto your grid pattern (see also FIG. 19-3).

Cut approximately a four-inch radius from the top of the rocker (inside radius) to the aft end, and at an overall length of 26 inches.

Clamp the rockers together and belt-sand their radii to conformity. Sand the surfaces smooth, leaving a slight radius on all sharp edges.

THE SEAT SUBASSEMBLY

Cut out the seat (F) and the back (G) as shown in FIGS. 19-6 and 19-7, leaving one edge of each piece beveled at 10 degrees. Sand their edges smooth. Sand radii along the front edge of the seat and curved top portion of the back to break their sharp corners.

Cut out two back support pieces (H) and two seat support pieces (J) from 5/8-inch × 3/4-inch oak. One end of each piece is to be radiused at 5/8-inch, with

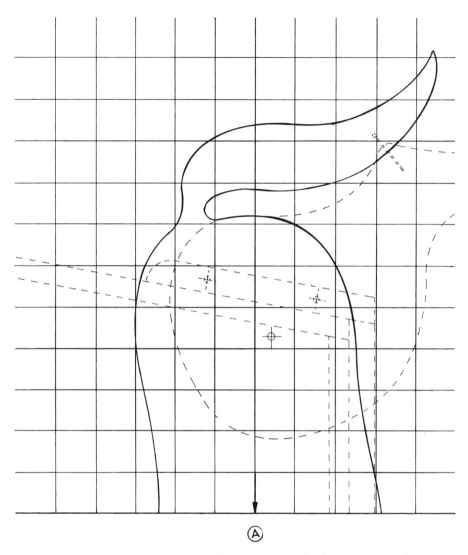

(A)

19-3 Align the two arrow points from this figure with the outline in FIG. 19-2 to make one complete body outline.

their opposite ends beveled at 10 degrees. These are neither right-hand nor left-hand at this point. Locate and drill through the 1/4-inch holes, as shown in FIG. 19-6. Countersink opposite surfaces of parts H and J, which are to become their inside surfaces upon assembly.

Align the appropriate support pieces with the edges of the seat and back, and glue and finish-nail them in place securely. Align the back with its supports along the aft edge of the seat with its supports. Using a finish nail as a "bit," drill through the lower ends of the back support pieces (H) and into the seat support pieces (J) about 1/4-inch. Apply wood glue to the mating surfaces between these

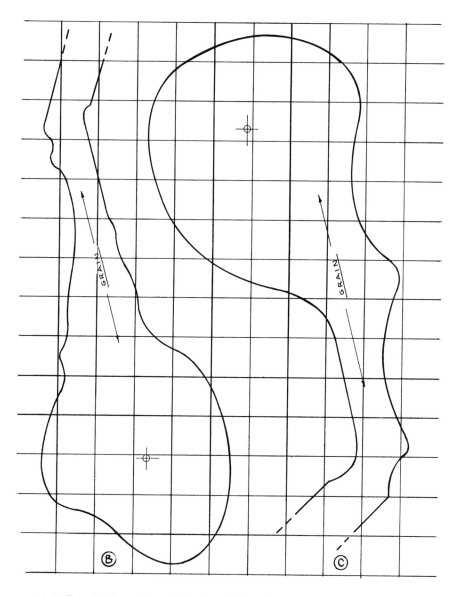

19-4 Transfer the outlines of the horse's legs, front and rear, onto your pattern.

components, and follow the pilot holes with finish nails and set them. The seat subassembly is now ready for final assembly.

THE TRAY SUBASSEMBLY

Cut out the tray piece (K) from a good grade of $1/2$-inch plywood. Cut out the aft and front support pieces (L and M) from oak. Contour the lower edge of piece L, as shown in FIG. 19-8, and cut a $1/4$-inch deep × $1/2$-inch-wide dado groove in it to

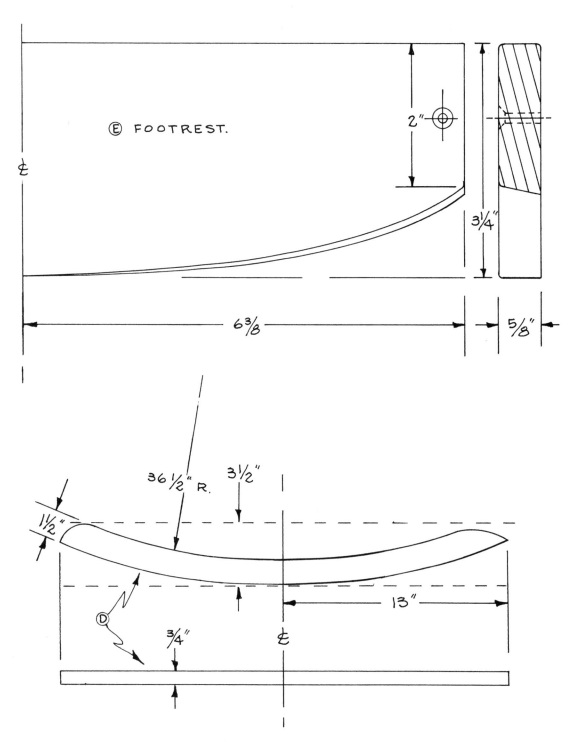

℄

Ⓔ FOOTREST.

2″

3¼″

6⅜

5⁄8″

36½″ R.   3½″

1½″

Ⓓ

¾″

℄

13″

19-5 Radius the front ends of these rockers at 1 1/2 inches.

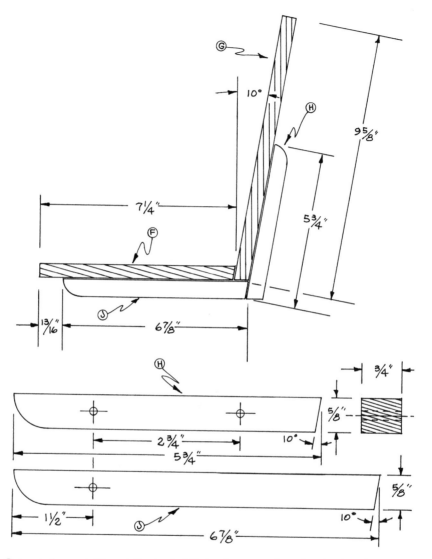

19-6 Cut out the seat (F) and the back (G), leaving one edge of each piece beveled at 10 degrees.

receive the aft edge of the tray (K). The contour makes for easier access and provides more leg room for the little jockeys. Radius all sharp exposed corners.

Apply glue to the dado cut and press the aft edge of the tray (K) in place. Align the front piece (M) with the front of the tray and pre-drill pilot holes for the finish nails, just deep enough to penetrate the tray. Apply wood glue to the mating surfaces and finish-nail these together.

Turn the tray subassembly upside down and locate four 1/2-inch × 1/2-inch 90-degree corner brackets on the under surface of the tray piece (K). One "leg" of each angle should be flush with the outside edge of the tray, and the other should

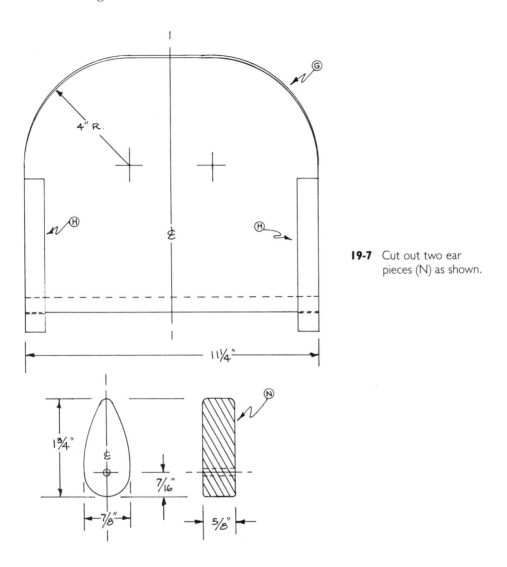

19-7 Cut out two ear pieces (N) as shown.

be flush against part L at the back or part M at the front. The tray subassembly is now ready for final assembly.

BODY ASSEMBLY

Choose the better surfaces of the body pieces (A) and the leg pieces (B and C) as their outside surfaces. Counterbore the attaching holes on the inside surfaces of the body parts (A) to accommodate a flat washer and 1/4-inch hex nut, about 1/4-inch deep. Drill through with a 1/4-inch drill for the 1/4-inch × 11/2-inch carriage bolts.

Lay a body piece (A) with its outside surface down on a clean workbench. Place the seat subassembly on the body and locate the screw hole centers in the body for the #8 × 11/4-inch flat head wood screws. Install these screws, temporar-

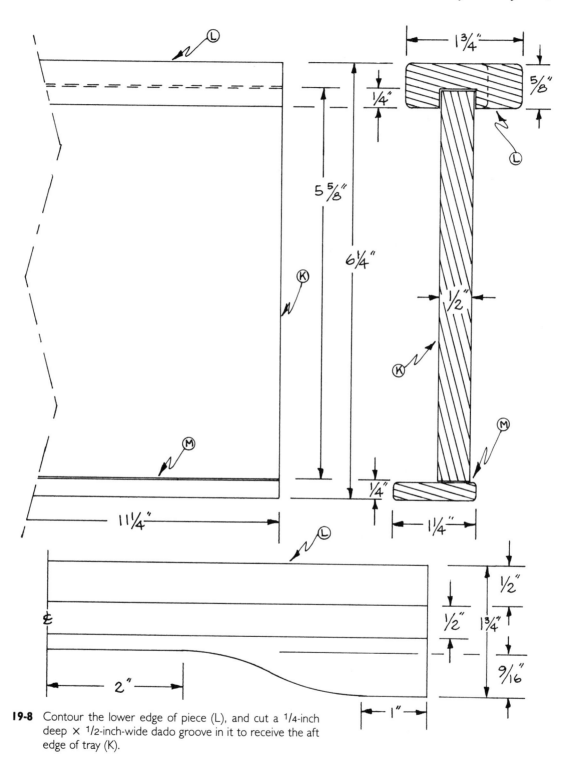

19-8 Contour the lower edge of piece (L), and cut a 1/4-inch deep × 1/2-inch-wide dado groove in it to receive the aft edge of tray (K).

ily for now. Place the tray subassembly in position and locate the pilot holes for the #6 × $1/2$-inch flat head retaining screws. Take care that the tray is $51/4$ inches above and in a parallel plane with the seat. Install the two retaining screws in the angle brackets.

Place the remaining body piece (A), outside surface down, on the bench. Position the assembly just completed onto it. Locate and drill the pilot holes for both the seat and tray subassemblies as before. Check for accurate and square alignment, and install the retaining screws.

INSTALLING THE LEGS AND ROCKERS

Pass a $1/4$-inch × $11/2$-inch carriage bolt through the hole previously drilled through the legs and into the matching holes in the body pieces (A), right and left. Install a flat washer and $1/4$-inch hex nut onto the bolts within the counterbored holes. Align the legs and snug these nuts up, temporarily. The horse should stand alone.

Place the rockers on the inside of the horse's hooves, right and left, and clamp them in place securely. Cut out the footrest piece (E) as shown in FIG. 19-5, and drill and countersink the two attaching holes. Fit it between the two front hooves and pilot-drill holes in the rockers for the two #8 × $11/4$-inch flat-head wood screws. Install the screws in place temporarily.

At this point you will want to enlist the aid of a wee bronc-buster as you establish the balance correctly and position the saddle over the center of gravity. Mark all the settings and separate the horse and rider for now—if you can—before proceeding further.

Drill through the rockers from their inside surfaces and slightly into the hooves. Countersink these holes in the rockers for the #8 × $11/4$-inch flat head wood screws. Trim the hooves to conform to the curvature of the rockers.

THE EARS AND TAIL

Cut out two ear pieces (N) as shown in FIG. 19-7. Drill through them for the #6 × $11/4$-inch round head wood screws. Radius the exposed corners of the ears and sand them smooth. It has been suggested that the ears might be fashioned out of leather, as a safer approach, if desired. Locate them on the horse's head and drill pilot holes for the two screws.

To lessen the chances of the tails being broken, drill through them at about a 30-degree angle so as to slightly penetrate the hocks using a small finish nail as a "bit." Apply a drop of glue within the approximately $1/4$-inch overlap and finish-nail securely.

NAIL ASSEMBLY

Disassemble all the matched and fitted components. Apply glue to all their mating surfaces and install them with the appropriate hardware permanently.

Ride 'em, cowboy!

20

Helmsman's wheel clock

This nautical piece is one which you can really take pride in building, owning, and showing off. The prototype was designed and built to function as a practical and decorative clock, but the first copy it inspired was constructed solely to serve as a decorative wall piece, period.

The woods chosen, and additional details which might be incorporated (carving, inlaying, etc.) can make this project a real work of art if you so choose. However, just following these instructions and the referenced illustrations will result in a beautiful and useful project which is comparatively easy to construct from readily available materials (FIG. 20-1).

The basic wheel components can be cut from standard $3/4$-inch lumber. The spokes and handles are turned from $3/4$-inch dowel rod stock, but you could also use more exotic woods throughout.

Twelve divisions of 30 degrees were used for two reasons. First, this makes the clock configuration layout a cinch. Secondly, adequate strength is thus provided to use this same basic design as a wine cart or a tea cart wheel.

INSTRUCTIONS

Start with the quadrants (A) which are to compose the basic wheel. Eight of these are required per wheel and can be cut from standard 1×4 ($3/4$-inch $\times 3^{1}/2$-inch) lumber as shown in FIG. 20-2. Each quadrant requires less than 10 linear inches. Pay particular attention to squaring their terminal ends to form two perfect circles of four pieces each, when glued end to end. Be sure to observe the direction of the grain.

THE WHEEL

Lay out the inside radii of the wheel quadrants (A) so as to leave a net after sanding of $5^{1}/4$ inches. Similarly, lay out the outside radii at about $7^{1}/16$ inches for the same reason. Fit them together and check for an accurate fit between the ends of the quadrants. Choose their better surfaces to be the outside (exposed) surfaces of the wheel.

Helmsman's Wheel Clock

Materials List

No. Req.	Part	Name	Thick	Wide	Long	Remarks
8	A	Wheel quadrant	3/4"	1 3/4"	10"	Cut from 3/4" × 3 1/2" × 10"
2	B	Hub section	3/4"	5" dia.		
1	C	Clock movement support	1/8"	4 3/4" dia.		1/8" plywood
12	D	Wheel spokes	3/4" dia.		3 5/8"	3/4" diameter dowel rod
12	E	Wheel handles	3/4" dia.		2 3/8"	

Hardware

2		Flat washers, 1/16" thick × (?) diameter* (Axle retainer/cover and spacer washer)
1		3/8" diameter rod stock, (?) long*
1		Clock movement, with hands
12		Numerals, I through XII
*		For cart wheel configuration, only—see text

Apply glue to the mating inside surfaces and to the mating ends, sparingly. Assemble these components so that the terminal ends of the quadrants of one circle overlap the quadrants of the other by 45 degrees, as shown in FIG. 20-2. Clamp these circular subassemblies together securely until the glue has set up properly.

Sand the outside diameter smoothly to bring it to a constant radius of 7 inches. This can be "roughed in" on a disc sander, then finish-sanded on a belt sander. Next, use a drum sander to bring the inside diameter into comformity at a smooth 5 1/4-inch radius. Sand the sharp corners into whatever uniform radius you want.

Locate and drill the twelve 3/8-inch-diameter by 3/8-inch-deep holes around the inside circumference at 30-degree intervals. These are to accommodate the twelve spoke pieces (D), as shown in FIGS. 20-3 and 20-4. Drill twelve similar holes around the outside circumference for the handle pieces (E). Their centerlines must be extensions of the same radii as for the inside (spoke) holes.

Omit this latter operation if you plan to use the wheel for a tea or wine cart application, which will be explained later.

THE SPOKES AND HANDLES

Referring to FIG. 20-5 turn out 12 spokes (D) and twelve handles (E), as shown. Both these parts were turned from 3/4-inch-diameter dowel rod for the prototype project. Sand these components smooth while they are still in the lathe.

20-1   Helmsman's wheel clock.

THE HUB

Cut out two circular hub pieces (B) from 3/4-inch material, five inches in diameter. Sand their edges and surfaces smooth. Radius the sharp corners but on the outside surfaces only, in the same manner as the wheel subassembly was radiused.

Align these two sections face to face, with their better surfaces outward. Rotate them so that their grain patterns are at right angles to each other, and clamp them securely together. (They will be glued together later.) Locate and drill the twelve 3/8-inch diameter holes, 1/2 inch deep, at 30-degree intervals as shown in FIG. 20-6.

Make the required cutout in these parts to accommodate the dimensions of whatever clock movement you have chosen.

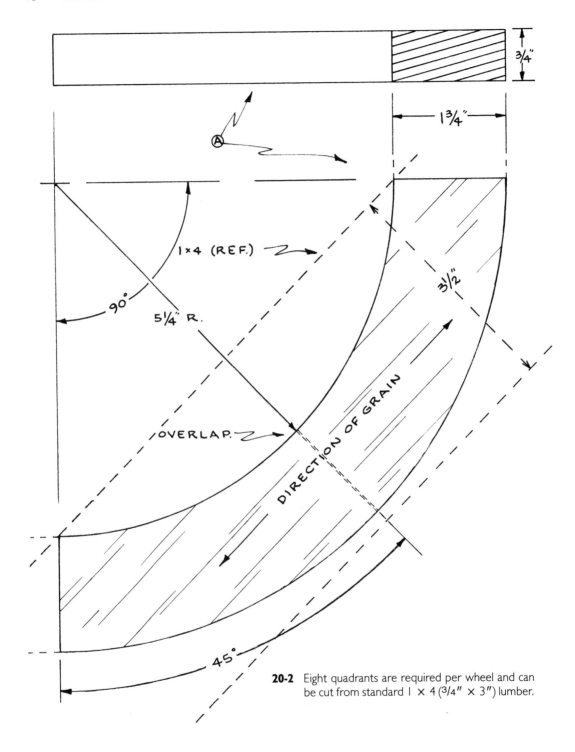

20-2 Eight quadrants are required per wheel and can be cut from standard 1 × 4 (3/4″ × 3″) lumber.

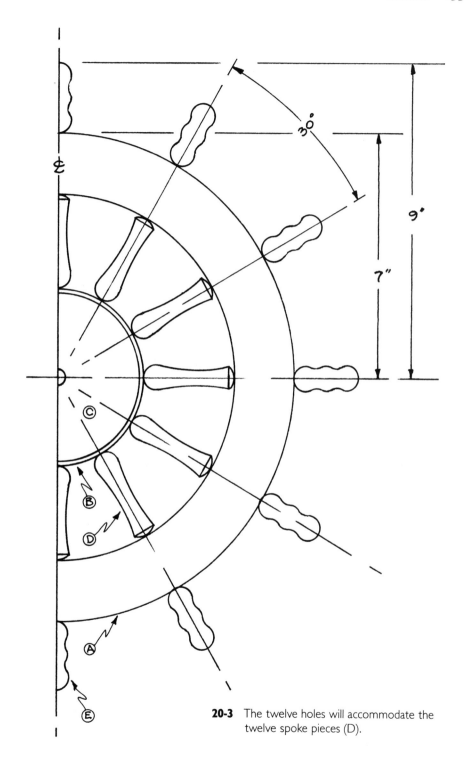

20-3 The twelve holes will accommodate the twelve spoke pieces (D).

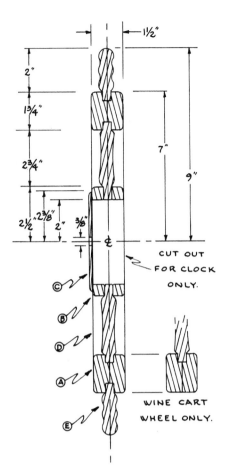

20-4 Note that different cuts depend on whether the end product will be a clock or a cart wheel.

CLOCK SUPPORT

Cut out a 4³/4-inch-diameter circle from ¹/8-inch plywood to make a part (C) clock movement support. Sand a radius around its circumference on one face, only, as shown in FIGS. 20-4 and FIG. 20-7.

In the clock configuration, drill a center hole to snugly accommodate the shaft diameter of the movement. Battery-operated clock movements are generally supported in place by this threaded shaft.

FINAL ASSEMBLY

Lay out the wheel subassembly with its back surface down, and on a flat workbench. Place the aft half of the hub (B) in its center, making sure that the wood grains have been indexed in their desired relationship. Apply wood glue to the ³/8-inch by ³/8-inch tenons of the spoke pieces (D), and press them into the previously drilled holes in the inside diameter of the wheel rim. Keep the spokes cor-

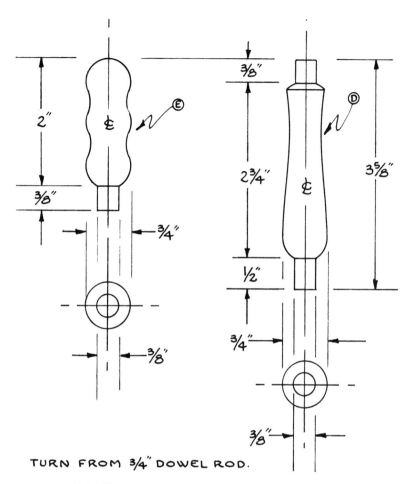

TURN FROM 3/4" DOWEL ROD.

20-5 Turn out twelve spokes (D) and twelve handles (E).

rectly aligned by nesting their 3/8-inch by 1/2-inch tenons into their respective half-holes in the aft hub piece.

Next, apply glue to the mating hub surfaces and to the remaining (inside) spoke tenons. Align the two hub halves correctly and press them together, locking in the spokes. Clamp the hub assembly together securely, and start installing the handles (E) in place around the wheel, applying glue to their tenons sparingly.

Align the clock movement support piece (C) concentrically with the outside surface of the hub and glue it in place, as shown in FIG. 20-4.

The completed wheel is now ready to receive whatever staining and/or coating(s) you want to give it. Once this is dry, the clock movement can be installed and the hands fitted in place on their shafts. You can buy attractive plastic numerals that are self-adhesive. I used Roman numerals in black and gold for the prototype clock.

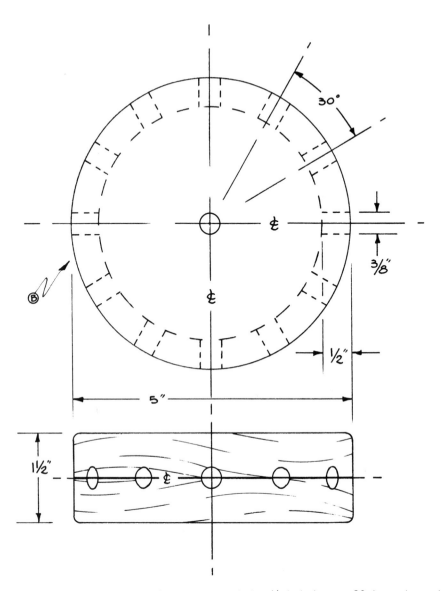

20-6   Locate and drill the twelve 3/8-inch diameter holes, 1/2 inch deep, at 30-degree intervals.

CART WHEELS

If the end items are to serve as cart wheels, drill a pilot hole through the centers of two aligned hub pieces (B). Counterbore the outside face of the hub to a depth of about 1/8 inch, and at a diameter to accommodate a suitable, thick washer. Follow the pilot hole through with a 3/8-inch-diameter bit, or whatever axle diameter has been chosen.

Drill through a washer so as to make its inside diameter a net fit of the shafting, and countersink this hole as shown in FIG. 20-7. Slip the washer over the

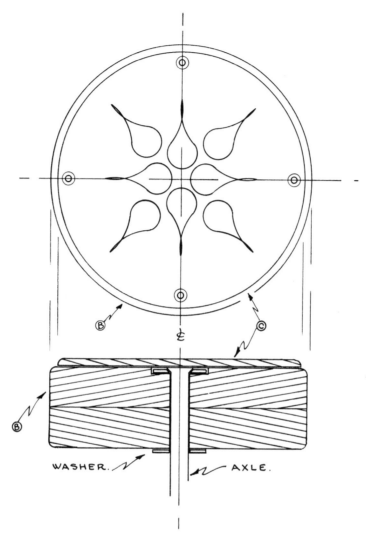

WASHER. AXLE.

20-7 Drill through a washer to make its inside diameter a net fit of the shafting, and countersink this hole.

squared end of the shaft and peen the shaft end so as to displace its material into the countersink. This procedure provides a very secure and thin "nut" on the axle ends. Most hardware stores carry short lengths of rod stock in various diameters. Alternatively, you can just cut off the head of a 3/8-inch-diameter bolt of a suitable length so that its "grip" (unthreaded portion) is about 1 1/2 inches. A couple of 3/8-inch hex nuts can then be used to mount such an independent axle onto whatever design.

When piece C is to serve as an axle retainer or cover, four screw holes should be located at 90-degree intervals, as shown in FIG. 20-7. Countersink these holes and use four oval-head Phillips screws to retain the cover in place on the hub.

Appendix

Shop notes

When you purchase a length of 2 × 4 lumber (or whatever dimension), you are also paying for the sawdust and planer chips that were removed from it at the sawmill. For instance, what passes for a "2 × 4" is actually reduced to $1^1/2$ inches thick by $3^1/2$ inches wide. That is what we have to work with.

For what to order, and what to expect, from your friendly neighborhood lumber dealer, please refer to FIG. A-1 and to the "standard sizes" tables. This information should help you buy the lumber you need for a particular project— and only what is needed. Standard lengths usually start at eight feet, increasing in increments of two feet beyond that, within limits.

In larger quantities, lumber is sometimes bought by the board foot. A *board foot* is a unit of measure equal to the cubic contents of a piece of lumber one foot square and one inch thick. Again, this isn't necessarily what you can expect to get for your money. The tables and FIG. A-2 should make this more understandable.

The kind and grade of the lumber to be purchased will be determined by the nature and requirements of the project to be undertaken. *Select* grades of lumber will have a few tight knots, while *clear* might have no knots at all. For exposed woodwork and finer woodworking projects, these grades are worth their higher prices. For ordinary construction, and where the lumber is to be filled and painted over, the *common* grades are usually adequate—and much less expensive.

PLYWOOD

A *sheet* of plywood usually refers to a piece of material 48 inches wide and 96 inches long. This excellent, laminated product is generally available in thicknesses of $1/4$ inch, $1/2$ inch, and $3/4$ inch, and in several grades. It is also available with hardwood veneer surface grains. When using plywood in a damp environment or where it will be exposed to moisture directly, choose exterior grades. Such grades have been laminated with water-proof glue.

Do not expect to get eight shelves from a sheet of plywood, each 12 inches wide and 48 inches in length. Unfortunately, the saw kerf has to be taken into consideration in all our plans. The *kerf* is the cut or incision made by a saw or other instrument. To put it another way, the kerf is the slot in your material that is left as

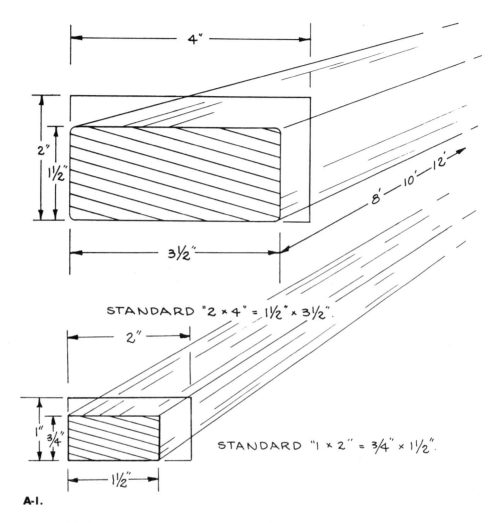

STANDARD "2 × 4" = 1½" × 3½".

STANDARD "1 × 2" = ¾" × 1½".

A-1.

the saw blade progresses through it. Thus, a 3/4-inch sheet of plywood, to become shelving, will yield eight shelves 11 7/8 inches wide and 47 7/8 inches long.

This doesn't mean that one can't cut shelves which are 12 inches wide, net, and a full four feet in length. It does mean that such planning, or lack of it, will substantially increase the cost of a given project—unless, of course, profitable use can be made of the material that is left.

When cutting components for a project the best results will be obtained by using a saw blade specifically designed for the purpose. The additional initial cost of a carbide tipped blade will be found to be a good investment.

CONSERVATION

Every effort has been made to utilize standard, generally available materials for the projects contained in this book, and to do so conservatively. We can't eliminate the fact of sawdust as a by-product of our craft, but creating needless waste and

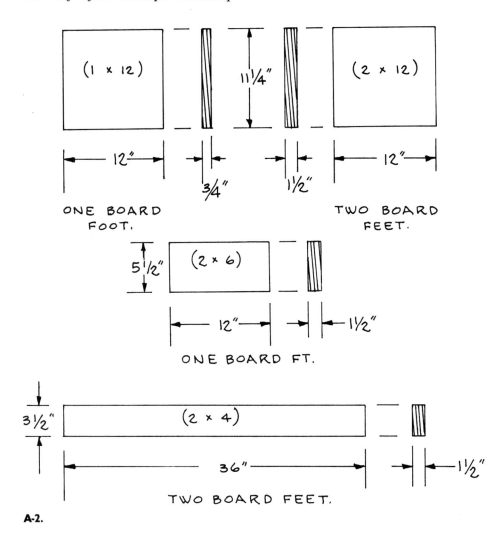

A-2.

Standard Lumber Sizes			Standard Lumber Sizes		
Designation	*Thick*	*Wide*	*Designation*	*Thick*	*Wide*
1 × 2	3/4″	1 1/2″	2 × 2	1 1/2″	1 1/2″
1 × 3	3/4″	2 1/2″	2 × 3	1 1/2″	2 1/2″
1 × 4	3/4″	3 1/2″	2 × 4	1 1/2″	3 1/2″
1 × 6	3/4″	5 1/2″	2 × 6	1 1/2″	5 1/2″
1 × 8	3/4″	7 1/4″	2 × 8	1 1/2″	7 1/4″
1 × 10	3/4″	9 1/4″	2 × 10	1 1/2″	9 1/4″
1 × 12	3/4″	11 1/4″	2 × 12	1 1/2″	11 1/4″

expense need not occur. (Refer to chapter 13, specifically FIG. 13-2, wherein the components for five child's chairs can be cut from a single sheet of 1/2-inch plywood.)

Before setting the dimensions for the components of a given project being designed, check first for the dimensions of the available materials to be used. It has been my experience that a fraction of an inch one way or another will seldom make any difference in the quality, utility, or appearance of the majority of projects.

Do not be too hasty to discard sound remnants of good materials left over from a project. It isn't scrap, per se, unless it can no longer be profitably used somewhere else. Some of the plans contained in this book require very little in the way of materials. This means that small pieces left over from larger projects can be turned to profit via the smaller ones. For instance, the largest piece in the ball gum dispenser project, chapter 15, is only 3/4-inch × 3¹/2 inches × 3¹/2 inches.

Gussets, cleats, glue blocks, etc. that will not show, even in a completed hardwood project, can be made from that which would otherwise become scrap.

JIGS AND POWER TOOL SETUPS

Try to avoid breaking down a setup for a particular cut or other operation until all components that require that operation have been processed. This is especially advisable when several of the same end item are to be built. In addition to saving both time and energy, this also assures greater interchangeability of components. It will pay off again during final assembly of a production run of like items.

Once a particular jig or setup has been made, try it first on a piece of scrap material—or at least on a piece of cheaper material. Check this test piece for dimensional accuracy before cutting into that prime oak, walnut, or mahogany— or even shelf pine, for that matter. Do remember to use a push stick to urge the workpiece through the saw blade, especially when working with the smaller pieces.

STOCK SHAPES AND SIZES

Figures A-3 and A-4 show some of the commonly available wood shapes and sizes that most of us just aren't equipped to turn out. It isn't feasible to try to compete with the molding mills and automatic lathes for many of the shapes that can add so much to our finished projects. You will find that these can be used singly or in various combinations to good effect (FIG. A-5).

DRILLING OPERATIONS

When an article or drawing calls for a 1/2-inch-diameter hole to be drilled to a depth of 5/8 inch into a 3/4-inch-thick piece of material, we know at once that it is to be a bottom-drilled hole. That is, at the indicated diameter and to the indicated depth, period. Conventional twist drill bits, wood bits, or paddle-blade bits cannot be used. These would drill the correct diameter all right, but their points would penetrate the opposite surface of the workpiece before reaching the required depth.

Check the relative merits and distinctive design features of the several bits available: twist, brad point, router, conventional wood, Forstner, etc. Some act as their own pilots, without the necessity of having first to drill a smaller pilot hole to prevent drift.

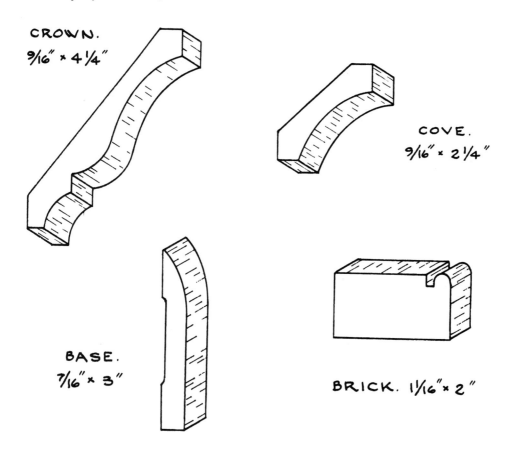

CROWN.
9/16" × 4 1/4"

COVE.
9/16" × 2 1/4"

BASE.
7/16" × 3"

BRICK. 1 1/16" × 2"

MOLDINGS.

A-3.

When drilling completely through a workpiece, you don't necessarily need a special bit. With the workpiece secured in place over a piece of scrap material, follow the pilot hole with the desired diameter bit until it begins to penetrate the scrap piece. This procedure will prevent the bit from mangling the opposite surface as it exits the workpiece.

An alternate procedure is to follow the pilot hole to a depth of no more than 3/4 the thickness of the workpiece. Then turn the piece over, completing the hole by following the pilot hole from the opposite surface until the desired diameters coincide within the workpiece. This results in a clean-cut circumference on both surfaces. Having to use "3/16-inch putty" in an attempt to conceal avoidable wounds isn't craftsmanship.

Exercise special care when drilling larger diameter holes with hole saws, and especially with the "out-rigger" type of fly cutters. Secure the workpiece to drill press table or workbench before beginning the cut.

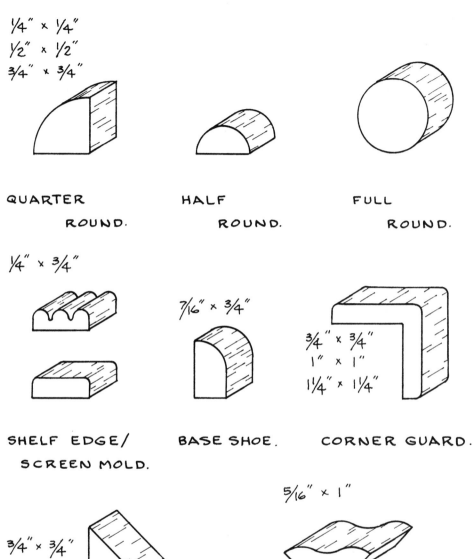

¼" × ¼"
½" × ½"
¾" × ¾"

QUARTER ROUND.

HALF ROUND.

FULL ROUND.

¼" × ¾"

7/16" × ¾"

¾" × ¾"
1" × 1"
1¼" × 1¼"

SHELF EDGE/ SCREEN MOLD.

BASE SHOE.

CORNER GUARD.

¾" × ¾"

5/16" × 1"

CHAMFER STRIP.

INSIDE CORNER.

A-4.

This final reminder: unless you follow good, safe shop practices, you might find yourself counting your fingers while trying to discover where the bench saw— or the drill press—threw the workpiece. I learned from a personal experience that it is unwise to attempt to brush an accumulation of chips from the immediate vicinity of an energized router bit! Accidents seldom "just happen." Most often they result from carelessness, haste, or from failure to exercise due caution.

A COMBINATION OF
STANDARD SHAPES
AND SIZES.

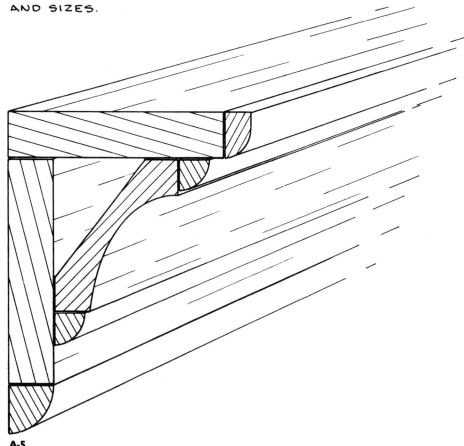

A-5.

Glossary

batten   a light strip of wood having an oblong cross section and used to fasten members of a structure together (FIG. G-1).

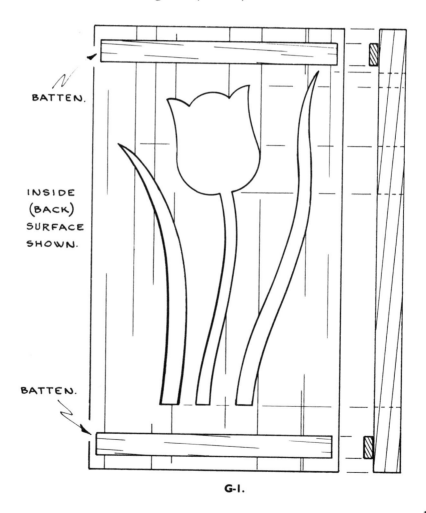

BATTEN.

INSIDE
(BACK)
SURFACE
SHOWN.

BATTEN.

G-1.

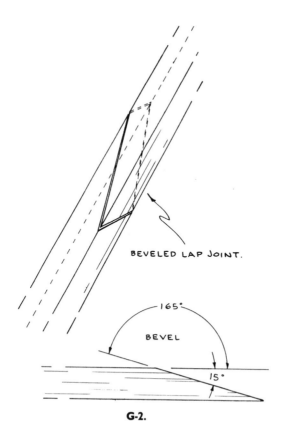

BEVELED LAP JOINT.

165°

BEVEL

15°

G-2.

bevel the inclination that one line or surface makes with another when not at right angles; to cut or slant at a bevel (FIG. G-2).

bit movable boring or drilling part (in many forms) used in a drill press, drill motor, or the like (FIG. G-3).

board foot a unit of measure equal to the contents of a piece of lumber one foot square and one inch thick (FIG. G-2).

bottom drill to plunge drill so as to bottom a hole in an unbroken circular plane and at right angles to the centerline of the hole (FIG. G-3).

chamfer an oblique surface cut on the edge or corner of a solid, usually a board, made by removing the arris (sharp ridge or corner) and usually sloping at 45 degrees (FIG. G-4).

concentric having a common center, usually of spheres and circles (FIG. G-5).

counterbore to drill to a larger diameter, concentric with an existing hole or bore, usually to a comparatively shallow depth (FIGS. G-5 and G-6).

countersink to enlarge the upper part of a hole or cavity by chamfering, to receive the cone-shaped head of a screw (FIG. G-6).

dado a groove recessed into one component so as to receive an adjoining component of corresponding (mating) dimensions (FIG. G-7).

dovetail a joining or fastening formed by one or more tenons and mortises spread in the shape of a dove's tail (FIG. G-8).

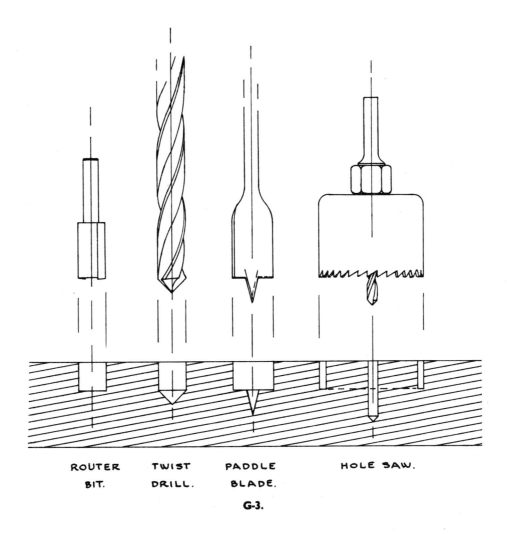

ROUTER   TWIST   PADDLE   HOLE SAW.
BIT.   DRILL.   BLADE.

G-3.

dowel a pin, usually round, fitting into corresponding holes in two adjacent pieces to align (and join) the two pieces (FIG. G-9).

flush even or level, as with a surface; in one plane.

fluting to form longitudinal flutes or furrows in; having flutes or grooves, as a pillar; act of making flutes (FIG. G-10).

gouge a chisel whose blade has a concave-convex cross section, the bevel being ground on either the inside or outside of the cutting end of the tool.

jig a device for holding the work in a machine tool; one for accurately guiding a drill or tool so as to ensure uniformity in successive pieces machined or cut.

kerf the cut or incision made by a saw or other instrument (FIG. G-11).

lap joint to join, as by scarfing, to form a single piece with the same dimensions throughout (FIG. G-2).

miter the abutting surface or bevel on either of the pieces joined in a miter joint (FIG. G-12).

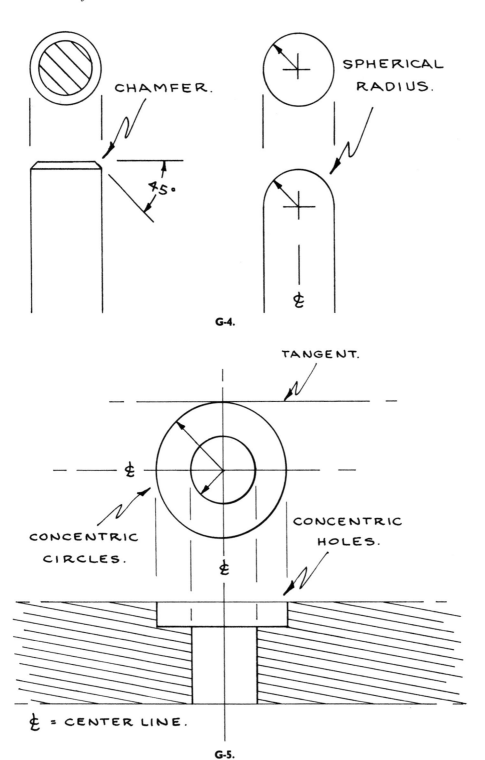

CHAMFER.

45°

SPHERICAL RADIUS.

₵

G-4.

TANGENT.

₵

CONCENTRIC CIRCLES.

CONCENTRIC HOLES.

₵

₵ = CENTER LINE.

G-5.

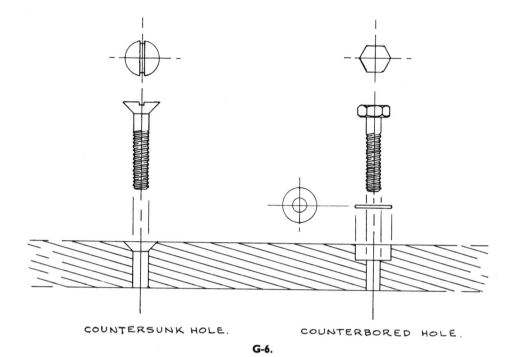

COUNTERSUNK HOLE.   COUNTERBORED HOLE.

G-6.

molding a decorative variety of contour or outline given to cornices, jambs, strips of woodwork, etc. (FIGS. G-3 and G-4).

mortise a rectangular cavity of considerable depth in one piece of wood to receive a corresponding projection (tenon) on another piece, so as to form a joint (FIG. G-13).

net fit secure engagement; exact, without slippage or free play.

parallel lines straight lines lying in the same plane but never meeting, no matter how far extended.

parallel planes planes having common perpendiculars, equidistant from one another, or others, at all corresponding points.

perpendicular vertical, upright; meeting a given line or surface at right angles.

rabbet a cut, groove, or recess made on the edge or surface of a board so as to receive the edge of an adjoining piece similarly cut (FIG. G-14).

radius a straight line extending from the center of a circle to its circumference, or, from the center of a sphere to its surface. To "radius" (verb) a sharp edge, corner or projection is to remove sufficient material therefrom as necessary to create a smoothly curving transition between adjacent surfaces, or to "break" an otherwise sharp corner, edge or projection on a piece of work.

reeding small convex semi-cylindrical molding resembling a reed, as on a column, where they resemble convex fluting (FIG. G-10).

sheet (*plywood*) usually a piece of laminated wood construction material, four feet wide by eight feet long, and available in several thicknesses.

skew a chisel having an oblique angle of cut; slanting.

spherical radius having the form of a sphere, usually a half-sphere, or hemisphere (FIG. G-4).

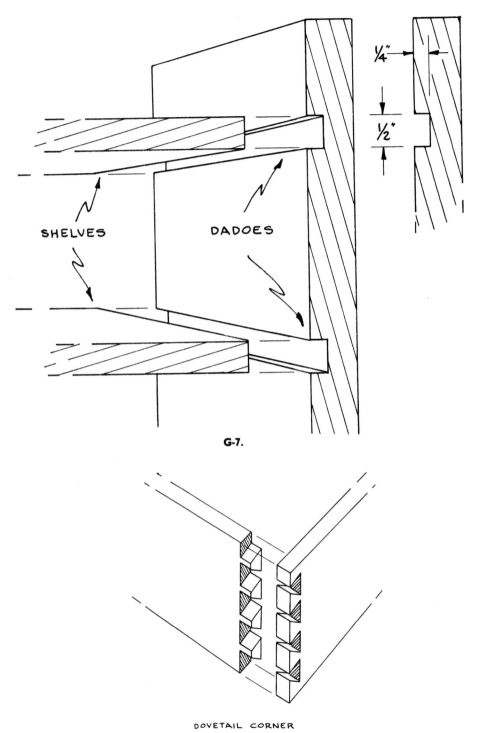

SHELVES   DADOES

¼"

½"

G-7.

DOVETAIL CORNER

G-8.

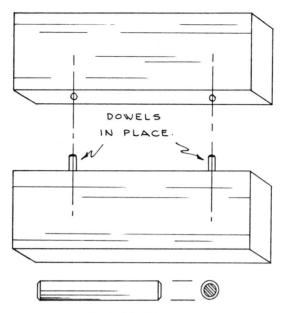

DOWELS
IN PLACE.

DOWEL PIN.

G-9.

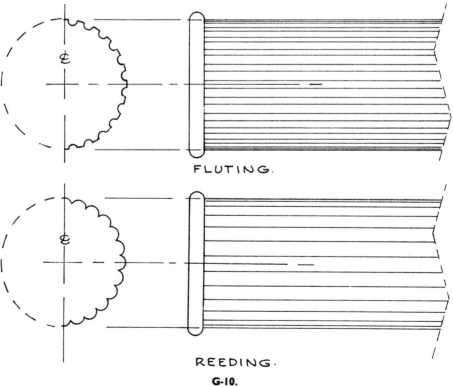

FLUTING.

REEDING.

G-10.

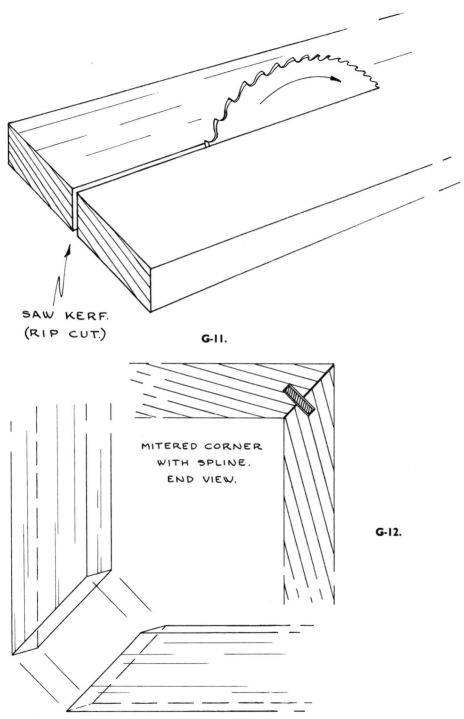

SAW KERF.
(RIP CUT.)

G-11.

MITERED CORNER
WITH SPLINE.
END VIEW.

G-12.

TWO PIECES MITER CUT 45 DEGREES
TO FORM A 90 DEGREE CORNER.

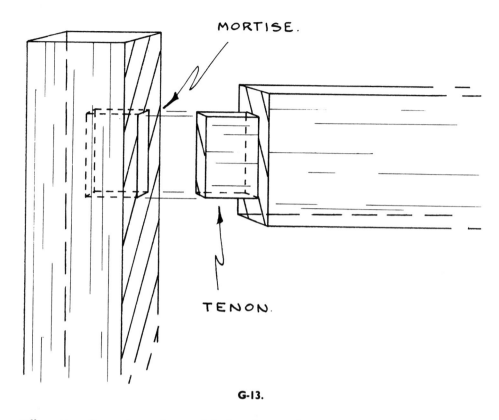

MORTISE.

TENON.

G-13.

splice to unite, as two pieces of timber, by overlapping and fastening their ends together (FIG. G-2).

spline a long, narrow, relatively thin strip of wood (FIG. G-12).

tangent touching; as a straight line in relation to a curve or surface (FIG. G-5).

tenon a projection fashioned on the end of a piece of wood, for insertion into a corresponding cavity (mortise) so as to form a joint (FIG. G-13).

tongue and groove a common joint consisting of a projecting strip (tongue) along the center of the edge or end of a board, and matching a groove in the edge of the next adjoining board (FIG. G-15).

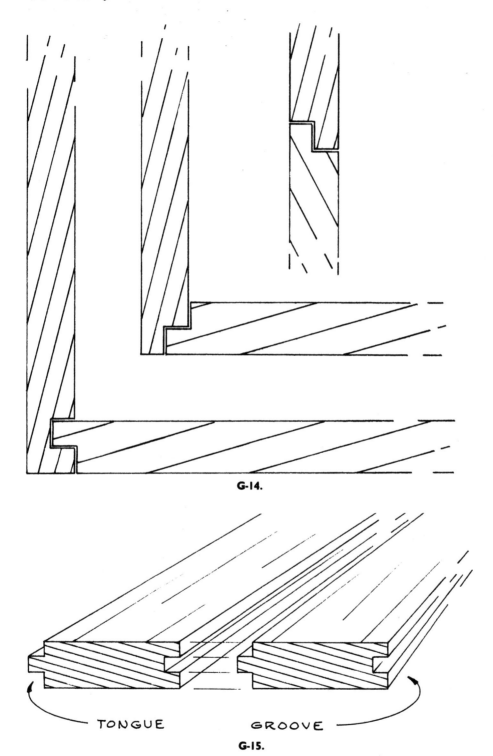

G-14.

TONGUE   GROOVE

G-15.

Index

Other Bestsellers
of Related Interest

ONE-WEEKEND COUNTRY FURNITURE PROJECTS—*Percy W. Blandford*

Transform simple materials into beautiful, functional objects with this brand-new selection of original projects to use in and around your home, in an easy, one-weekend format, especially for time-conscious hobbyists. A basic understanding of woodworking techniques is all you need to build an attractive, durable piece of furniture in as little as 12 hours. You get nearly 50 original project plans—all requiring only simple hand tools and inexpensive materials—and ample drawings and instructions for every design. 240 pages, 163 illustrations. Book No. 3702, $14.95 paperback, $24.95 hardcover

KATHY LAMANCUSA'S GUIDE TO WREATH MAKING—*Kathy Lamancusa, C.P.D.*

Now, you can enjoy the inviting charm of hand-crafted wreaths in your home all year long. Lamancusa clearly explains the most intricate aspects of wreath making. Beginning with the basics, you'll look at the materials used in wreath making with instructions for locating, cutting, and combining them. Then you'll move on to such projects as bows, kitchen wreaths, seasonal wreaths, wreaths for children, romantic wreaths, masculine wreaths, special occasion wreaths. 128 pages, 133 illustrations. Book No. 3492, $10.95 paperback, $19.95 hardcover

KATHY LAMANCUSA'S GUIDE TO FLORAL DESIGN—*Kathy Lamancusa, C.P.D.*

Create exquisite silk and dried floral designs for *every* room of your home with this easy-to-follow guide. You'll learn to work with the various materials and supplies and master basic design techniques quickly and easily with step-by-step photographs and instructions. Then you'll go beyond the legendary techniques to create fresher, more modern styles. Projects include wall and table arrangements, baskets, and special occasion designs. 128 pages, 166 illustrations. Book No. 3491, $12.95 paperback, $21.95 hardcover

THE DRILL PRESS BOOK: Including 80 Jigs and Accessories to Make—*R. J. De Cristoforo*

The drill press, after the table saw, is the second most important tool in the workshop. In this well-illustrated guide, you'll discover unique ways to develop the tool's potential in over 80 project plans. As De Cristoforo guides you through each application of this versatile tool, you'll benefit from hundreds of hints based on his years of woodworking experience. 304 pages, 406 illustrations. Book No. 3609, $16.95 paperback, $25.95 hardcover

CRAFTS FOR KIDS: A Month-By-Month Idea Book—2nd Edition—*Barbara L. Dondiego*
Illustrations by Jacqueline Cawley

Packed with dozens of project ideas, this collection of simple and inexpensive crafts is great for teaching children ages, preschool through elementary, about colors, shapes, numbers, and letters, as well as aiding them in their development of hand-eye coordination and motor skills. This revised edition features 20 all-new projects, including crafts for all major holidays, gift-giving, and cooking crafts. 240 pages, 164 illustrations. Book No. 3573, $14.95 paperback only

DESIGNING AND CONSTRUCTING MOBILES—*Jack Wiley*

Discover the fun and satisfaction of learning to create exciting mobile art forms . . . to add a personal decorator touch to your home, as unique craft projects for school class or club, even as a new income source! All the skills and techniques are here for the taking in this excellent, step-by-step guide to designing and constructing mobiles from paper, wood, metals, plastic, and other materials. 224 pages, 281 illustrations. Book No. 1839, $19.95 hardcover only

FRAMES AND FRAMING: The Ultimate Illustrated How-to-Do-It Guide
—*Gerald F. Laird and Louise Meiere Dunn, CPF*

This illustrated step-by-step guide gives complete instructions and helpful illustrations on how to cut mats, choose materials, and achieve attractively framed art. Filled with photographs and eight pages of full color, this book shows why a frame's purpose is to enhance, support, and protect the artwork, and never call attention to itself. You can learn how to make a beautiful frame that complements artwork. 208 pages, 264 illustrations. Book No. 2909, $13.95 paperback only

UPHOLSTERY TECHNIQUES ILLUSTRATED
—*W. Lloyd Gheen*

"... packed with information that isn't available in other ordinary upholstery handbooks ..."
—***Antiques Dealer***

This guide covers everything from stripping off old covers and padding to restoring and installing new foundations, stuffing, cushions, and covers. The most up-to-date pro techniques are included along with time- and money-saving "tricks-of-the-trade" not usually shared by professional upholsterers. 350 pages, 549 illustrations. Book No. 2602, $17.95 paperback only